KU-756-932

GUIDE TO INFORMATION SOURCES IN ALTERNATIVE THERAPY

Guide to
Information Sources in Alternative Therapy

Barbara Allan

THE BRITISH SCHOOL OF O.
1-4 SUFFOLK ST., LONDON SW1Y 4HG
TEL: 01 - 930 9254-8

Gower

Aldershot · Brookfield USA · Hong Kong · Singapore · Sydney

© Barbara Allan 1988

All rights reserved. No part of this publication may be reproduced, stored in a retrieval system, or transmitted in any form or by any means, electronic, mechanical, photocopying, recording, or otherwise without the prior permission of Gower Publishing Company Limited.

Published by Gower Publishing Company Limited
Gower House
Croft Road
Aldershot
Hants GU11 3HR
England

Gower Publishing Company
Old Post Road
Brookfield
Vermont 05036
USA

British Library Cataloguing in Publication Data
Allan, Barbara
    Guide to information sources in alternative
    therapy.
    1. Man. Therapy. Alternative methods.
    Information sources
    I. Title
    615.5'07

Library of Congress Cataloging-in-Publication Data
Allan, Barbara (Barbara C.)
    Guide to information sources in alternative therapy/Barbara Allan.
    p.   cm.
    Bibliography: p.
    Includes index.
    1. Alternative medicine—Bibliography.   2. Alternative medicine—
Information services.   3. Searching, Bibliographical.   I. Title.
    Z6675.A42A43   1988
    [R733]
    016.6158—dc19   88–10530 CIP

ISBN 0–566–05611–9

Printed and bound in Great Britain by
Anchor Brendon Ltd, Tiptree, Essex

Contents

Contents

Figures

Tables

PART I
INFORMATION SOURCES IN ALTERNATIVE THERAPY

1

Introduction

INTRODUCTION

The purpose of this book is to help those who are involved in or are interested in alternative therapy to find the information that they need.

What is 'alternative therapy'?

The phrase is used to describe a range of therapeutic practices which facilitate personal growth and development. Practitioners who offer these skills frequently work outside traditional organizations and they are likely to have obtained their professional qualifications and training by attending independent educational bodies rather than polytechnics or universities. Examples of alternative therapy include: co-counselling; bioenergetics; dance therapy and Reichian therapy. A full list of the alternative therapies covered in depth in this book is given later in this chapter.

How does 'alternative therapy' differ from 'alternative medicine'?

In practice, it is virtually impossible to separate the therapies into two groups as they tend to have a similar aim – to improve the physical, emotional, intellectual, psychic or spiritual well-being of a person. For the purposes of this book, attention is focused on those therapies which are primarily concerned with physical, emotional, psychic and spiritual development. Where therapies

3

based on working at a physical level have been included it is because these therapies are used to facilitate personal development as well as heal physical ailments – though it is recognized that these two applications are not exclusive.

Information needs

The aim of this book is to provide a useful resource which can be used by people looking for information in the field of alternative therapy.

Many different groups of people may be involved in alternative therapy:

Practitioner therapists and counsellors – in the private and public sectors

Trainers and educators in this field

Health services personnel, for example nurse tutors, psychologists

Social services personnel, for example social workers, probation officers

Education staff, for example student counsellors

Students in the above fields

Librarians and information scientists

Clients of alternative therapists

General public.

These categories are not exclusive, a practitioner therapist can also be a trainer in this field, but they do indicate that the information needs of the various groups of people involved in alternative therapy are likely to vary enormously:

A practitioner may be looking for a source of aromatherapy oils.

A trainer may be looking for videotapes to demonstrate a particular point.

A workshop administrator may be looking for a conference centre with a particular set of facilities in a particular part of the country.

A member of the public may want to find out what therapy is about.

A librarian may be asked to provide a detailed reading list on drama therapy.

It would be impossible to write a book which would satisfy the needs of all the people searching for information on alternative therapy. This book is *not* an exhaustive bibliography on this subject – its purpose is to guide the reader through the literature on alternative therapy and to provide examples which are likely to be readily accessible to the information seeker. The book gives general guidelines to searching for information and includes examples of sources which I have found most helpful in my various searches for information in this field.

STRUCTURE OF THE BOOK

This book is divided into three parts.

Part I   Information sources in alternative therapy

This introduction is followed by a description of alternative therapy, its history and development and the relationships which exist between the different kinds of therapy (Chapter 2). There is then a description of sources of information (libraries, bookshops and publishers) and an overview of different types of materials (printed, audiovisual and computer-based sources).

Chapter 4 considers searching for information and covers the search strategy and different types of searches (searching for people or organizations, manual searches and computerized searches). Special emphasis is placed on searching the abstracting and indexing journals and computerized searching.

Part II   The information sources: a bibliography

Part II begins with a bibliography of general sources, that is, those which may contain information about one or more therapies (Chapter 5). The bibliography has the following layout:

Printed sources
Reference items
   Guides to
     libraries

    bookshops
    publishers
  Literature guides
  Dictionaries
  Encyclopedias
  Directories
  Bibliographies
Abstracting and indexing journals
Periodicals
Official publications
Research publications

Audiovisual resources
Film and video
Cassettes and records

Computerized resources
On-line databases
CD-ROM
Videotex

This is followed by a detailed bibliography on different types of alternative therapy arranged in alphabetical order by subject as shown in Table 1.1.

It was originally proposed to group the alternative therapies according to the level at which they act on an individual, that is, physical therapies, psychological therapies and spiritual therapies. The literature already appears to fall into these categories and many books and organizations use this method of classification of the alternative therapies. A closer examination of the subject field showed that an ever-growing number of therapies did not fit into these neat categories.

For example: some of the physical therapies also work at a psychological level; astrology can be used at both psychological and spiritual levels; dream therapy can work at a transpersonal level. Also, new therapies and newer versions of established ones are constantly emerging which may not fit into these neat categories, and many therapists and healers are now eclectic in their approach and are likely to offer their own mixture of a variety of therapies which may work at different levels.

Table 1.1   Alphabetical listing of the alternative therapies

Acupressure
Alexander technique
Aromatherapy
Art therapy
Astrological counselling
Bodymind therapies
Colour therapy
Co-counselling
Crystal healing
Dance therapy
Drama therapy
Dream therapy
Feldenkrais technique
Gestalt therapy
Hypnotherapy
Massage therapy
Meditation
Metamorphic technique, reflexology, zone therapy
Music therapy
Neurolinguistic programming
Polarity therapy
Primal therapy
Psychodrama
Psychosynthesis
Rebirthing
Reichian therapy
Reiki
Rolfing
Shamanism
Shiatsu massage
Spiritual healing
T'ai chi
Traditional healing
Yoga

Part III   People, organizations and activities

Chapter 9 provides details on how to find information about:

People, for example, practitioners, trainers, authors
Informal groups and networks
Societies and associations

Therapy centres
Current activities, for example, workshops and training courses.

HOW TO USE THIS BOOK

The book aims to provide a useful resource which can be used by people looking for information in the field of alternative therapy.

Chapter 2 provides a brief introduction for those who are new to the field of alternative therapy.

If you are unfamiliar with the processes involved in searching for information, I suggest that you start by reading Chapters 3 and 4.

Those interested in finding information on a known therapy should consult the index to find where that therapy is covered in depth. If you are unable to find what you are looking for, refer to the general sources in Chapter 5.

Those looking for a particular type of information product such as videotapes should look in the relevant section in Chapter 5 and also under specific therapies.

This book uses two arrangements for the references and source materials.

In the 'References' section at the end of Chapter 2 and the individual 'Books' sections in Chapters 6 to 8, a standard biblio-graphical arrangement has been adopted, that is, alphabetically by author or editor. Works by the same person appear chronologically, with two or more works published in the same year appearing alphabetically by title. Works written by an author (or editor) jointly with another follow the works written by that person alone. Each reference gives the following information:

Author(s) or editor(s), year, title, publisher, place.

Contributed works appear in quotation marks, followed by the name of the editor of the volume of which they appear, with the title of the volume (or journal) in italics.

All other references in this book have been arranged in alpha-betical order by title taken in word by word order and ignoring prefixes such as 'a' and 'the'. Each reference contains the following information:

Title. Edition. Author or editor (Place: Publisher, Date). Frequency.

Where I have been able to obtain a copy of the item I have annotated the reference. For some items (particularly of USA origin) this has been impossible and I have relied on annotations from works such as *The Whole Again Resource Guide* and specialized bibliographies and catalogues. In a few cases I have been able to track down a reference in one source only, and I have been unable either to see the original item or find out more about it – rather than omit these items they have been included without annotation.

The printed, audiovisual and computerized resources covered in this book are primarily written or produced in English and most originate from the UK or USA. Organizations mentioned in the book are also primarily found in the UK or USA. Guidance to items and organizations from other countries is given in Chapters 5 and 9.

Finally, this literature guide does not attempt to provide a comprehensive resource listing of all items published or relevant to the field of alternative therapy. Rather, this work can be used as a starting point to finding the required information or resources.

2

Introduction to alternative therapy

THE SCOPE OF THE ALTERNATIVE THERAPIES

Therapy can be described as a process which enables people to become 'more themselves' and in touch with their own processes and power. Different forms of therapy offer the opportunity for this to take place in different ways: via the body through massage or dance; via the emotions through counselling and catharsis; by working at an explicitly subconscious level through guided meditations or hypnosis; or at a psychic level by aura cleansing and balancing. Most forms of therapy work at a number of different levels at the same time and many therapists are eclectic in their approach.

Therapy as a process is probably as old as the human race and was at one time an integral part of life, being found in many rituals, customs and practices. For example: many Eastern religions incorporate practices, now identified as therapeutic, which are thousands of years old; North American native Indian cultures and practices are also 'therapeutic'. In the West, therapy as a 'subject' has existed since the mid-nineteenth century and can be linked to industrialization, the decline of traditional religions, and the departmentalization of modern life. Indeed, therapists today have taken over (to a certain extent) the roles of shaman, priest and priestess, wise woman, and witch. This link is reflected in the therapy literature, which extends from the fields of medicine and psychology to anthropology and religion.

Wilber (1979, 1980, 1981) has described the field of personal development in some detail and it can be divided into three broad

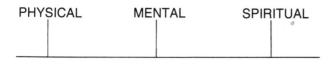

PHYSICAL   MENTAL   SPIRITUAL

Figure. 2.1   Human development

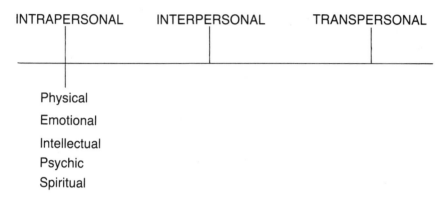

INTRAPERSONAL   INTERPERSONAL   TRANSPERSONAL

Physical

Emotional

Intellectual

Psychic

Spiritual

Figure. 2.2   Personal development and the world

areas: physical, mental and spiritual. This is shown in Figures 2.1 and 2.2. The alternative therapies considered in this book work on either one or more levels of development. Indeed, the three levels are intrinsically linked as changes at one level will affect the others. The division of the therapies into these three fields is given below but it should be noted that this is not a comprehensive listing of the therapies covered in this book.

Physical therapies
Manipulative therapies: Alexander and Feldenkrais techniques, rolfing, reflexology.
Oriental therapies: Shiatsu and acupressure.
Exercise/movement therapies: dance, T'ai chi, yoga.
Sensory therapies: colour, art, music.

Included in the physical therapies are also systems of medicine (acupuncture, anthroposophical medicine, homeopathy), nutrition (clinical nutrition) and healing substances (flower remedies, herbal medicine and crystal essences). These particular therapies are not considered in this book.

Psychological therapies
Analytic therapies: Freudian and neo-Freudian analysis; Jungian
    analysis.
Humanistic therapies: co-counselling; gestalt; primal; rebirthing.
Relaxation techniques: meditation; guided imagery.

The analytic therapies are not considered in this book except in
their historical context.

Spiritual therapies
Transpersonal psychologies: psychosynthesis.
Transpersonal approaches: spiritual healing; some traditional
    systems of medicine.

Spiritual therapies which are closely associated with a particular
system of religion such as Sufism and Kabbalah are not considered
in this book.

Some of the alternative therapies are frequently grouped together
under the heading 'humanistic psychology', which is a phrase used
to describe and distinguish a wide range of methods and approaches
to personal growth and development. Humanistic approaches
recognize the importance of:

Personal responsibility
Self-direction
Expanding awareness at all levels
Encouragement towards mutual collaboration.

Humanistic approaches include the following areas of concern: the
integration of body, mind and soul where each relates to and inter-
acts with other dimensions of personal life and each contributes to
the well-being and functioning of the individual. They encourage
the reintegration of these elements of human experience and the
development of the unity of the individual. This approach also
looks at individuals in the world where they too function at three
levels: as an individual personality; in activities with others; and in
contact with wider questions and transpersonal dimensions of
human experiences. Different humanistic approaches may emphasize different aspects and levels of personal growth. These aspects
of humanistic psychologies are described in IDHP (1986).
    Rowan (1983) places humanistic psychology in between Wilber's

mental and spiritual levels of personal development and states that they are quite different from transpersonal psychology on one side and psychoanalysis and behaviourism on the other. In this

Table 2.1   A summary of the alternative therapies covered in this book

Therapy	Main modes of action		
	Physical	*Psychological*	*Spiritual*
Acupressure	+		
Alexander technique	+		
Aromatherapy	+		
Art therapy		+	+
Astrological counselling		+	+
Bodymind therapies	+	+	+
Colour therapy			+
Co-counselling		+	
Crystal healing			+
Dance therapy		+	+
Drama therapy		+	
Dream therapy		+	+
Feldenkrais technique	+		
Gestalt therapy		+	
Hypnotherapy		+	+
Massage therapy	+		
Meditation		+	+
Metamorphic technique etc.	+		
Music therapy		+	+
Neurolinguistic programming		+	
Polarity therapy	+		
Primal therapy		+	
Psychodrama		+	
Psychosynthesis		+	+
Rebirthing	+	+	
Reichian therapy	+	+	
Reiki	+	+	+
Rolfing	+		
Shamanism	+	+	+
Shiatsu massage	+		
Spiritual healing		+	+
T'ai chi	+	+	+
Traditional healing	+	+	+
Yoga	+	+	+

book the alternative therapies include those which fall neatly under the heading of humanistic psychology and also other therapies which fall into the physical and spiritual levels of development. This is summarized in Table 2.1.

As individuals move through the levels to the spiritual level (this movement is not necessarily linear and may be multidimensional) their level of consciousness expands and they become increasingly aware of what Heron (1987) has described as 'the other world'. By this he means:

> a non-physical, non-subjective realm of places, powers and presences that has spatial, temporal and energetic properties that is in some respects independent of the physical world and in other respects is in continuous interaction with it.

Heron uses a range of different terms to refer to this realm: the other world; the subtle universe; the matrix world; the inner world; the tacit universe; the occult world. This 'world' can be contacted through many different alternative therapies and particularly through meditation and yoga. Some therapies, such as crystal therapy, explicitly evoke this other world while Mindell's (1984) dreamsbody appears to be rooted in it. Traditional medicine and spiritual healing are also frequently staged in this other world. Heron provides a very vivid personal account of living at the interface between this world and another reality. While some of his ideas may appear quite esoteric to some readers, they do have practical applications at a more mundane level. An example given in his book is that of charismatic training, which is the cultivation of presence in interaction with others.

ALTERNATIVE THERAPIES AND OTHER SUBJECTS

Figure 2.3 indicates how the field of alternative therapy is connected to other subject areas. Some of these connections are fairly obvious while others may appear to be obscure. The links between alternative therapies and all these different subject fields vary: some are strong, others weaker. An example of a weak link is the connection with psychiatry, which includes psychoanalysis, while a strong connection can be seen between some alternative therapies (art, drama, psychodrama, music) and the creative arts. One difficulty in attempting to impose an academic classification is that many attributes of eclectic alternative therapy may include processes and activities which are part of other subject areas such as the creative arts. This indicates that, to some extent, the alternative therapies (which are focused on personal change and growth) are a special example of a process which happens during everyone's life.

What makes the alternative therapies 'special' is that they involve a person consulting a therapist for help in the normal processes of growth or change. This 'help' may be asked for at a stage when the process appears to be stuck, or is extremely painful and extra help and support is needed, or it may be that the person wants to speed up and broaden his or her normal life processes. Two helpful descriptions of this process have been described by Ernst and Goodison (1981) and Rowan (1983).

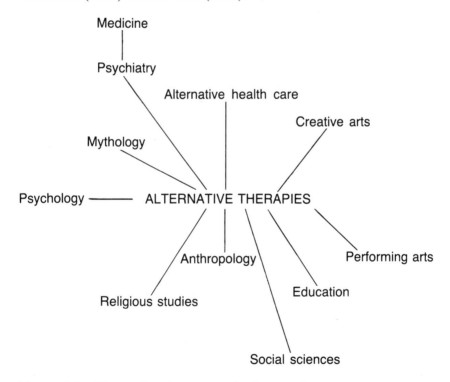

Figure 2.3 Alternative therapy and other subject areas

Milroy (1985) provides an interesting description of the role of the therapist:

> All the therapist – of whatever persuasion, shape or colour – can do, is provide assistance, support, feedback, advice and a range of tricks of varying efficacy. The bottom line in therapy is that the client must heal themselves. . . .

HISTORICAL PERSPECTIVE

Today there are many different kinds of alternative therapy, and common therapies are described in Part II. New therapies are constantly emerging. What follows looks at some of the links between different forms of therapy and sets them in a broader context.

Figure 2.3 indicates the depth and the breadth of the subjects linked to the alternative therapies. Indeed, the diagram can be expanded to include subjects such as linguistics and computer science (which were used in the development of neurolinguistic programming) and post-Einstein physics (which has been used by people looking at the links between therapy, Buddhism and physics). The figure also indicates that the roots of the alternative therapies are varied and in some cases extremely old. Kovel (1978) divides both mainstream and alternative therapies into the following groups:

Analytic therapies
Post-analytic therapies: the human potential movement
The social dimensions: group approaches
Behavioural directive therapies.

These are outlined in more detail in Table 2.2.

The analytic therapies include Freudian analysis, psychoanalytic psychotherapy, and also the neo-Freudian therapies as practised by Adler, Rank, Horney, Sullivan, Fromm and others who diverged from some of Freud's beliefs. These analytic therapies are not covered in this book as they are considered mainstream therapy but their work is still relevant to some alternative therapists: a

Table 2.2   Kovel's classification of mainstream and alternative therapies

---

Analytic therapies
Freudian psychoanalysis and psychoanalytical psychotherapy
Neo-Freudian analysis
Jung and analytical psychology
The existential approach

The post-analytic therapies: the human potential movement
Rogerian therapy
Gestalt therapy
Biofunctional therapies
  Reichian therapy, bioenergetics
Primal therapy
Mysticotranscendent approach

The social dimensions: group approaches
Traditional group therapy
Encounter groups
Est
Psychodrama
Transactional analysis
Family therapy

Behavioural directive therapies
Somatic therapy
Sex therapy
Directive therapy: hypnotherapy, reality therapy
Rational-emotive therapy
Behaviour therapy

---

recent publication by workers at the Women's Therapy Centre in London cites Freud and others (Ernst and Maguire (1987)).

Jung's work has been used by both traditional and many alternative therapists: his ideas on the transpersonal, archetypes, symbols, and spirituality can be seen in the work of art and dream therapists, astrological counsellors and others. The work of existentialists is perhaps highlighted by the ideas and works (including poetry) of Laing who, in the 1960s, took a radical approach to psychiatry and helped to create an anti-psychiatry movement which in turn fed into the alternative therapy movement.

The human potential movement really flourished in the 1960s

17

and 1970s, and has been described by Rowan (1976) and Kovel. Carl Rogers played an important part in this revolution by developing Rogerian counselling, 'which provided a workable clearly defined psychotherapeutic approach based on humanist-existential principles'. The ideas developed by Rogers are incorporated into many alternative therapies and some references to his work are included at the end of this chapter. At about the same time Perls devised gestalt therapy, which looks at the whole being and attempts to increase the client's awareness of the here and now. Gestalt therapy is included in Part II as it is included in the work and training programmes of many alternative therapists.

The biofunctional therapies include Reich's work, which marked a very important step: from the mind to the body. Reichian therapy includes focusing on 'body armour', which represents emotional blocks bound up in the body. Reich was very concerned with a physical energy-flow which he labelled 'orgone energy'. His method of treatment is sometimes called orgone therapy. Boadella (1985) described the work and controversies which surrounded Reich, and sets it in the context of the social and political setting of this century.

Reich's work was taken up by Lowen who helped develop the field of bioenergetics. Both Reichian therapy and bioenergetics are considered to be alternative therapies and so are covered in Part II. Their work has been developed by therapists such as Boadella, Mindell and Keleman, whose work is covered in the section in Chapter 6 on bodymind therapies.

Another strand of development took place in the 1960s and 1970s when Dr Arthur Janov developed primal therapy, which focuses on helping clients to express their deepest feelings. Kovel provides a good overview of primal therapy and it is covered later in this book.

The mysticotranscendent approaches attempt to use a combination of therapy and transcendent approaches to enable people to attain a different level of consciousness and transcend their personality and so achieve oneness with the cosmos. Many of these approaches are centuries old and Eastern in origin. Transcendent approaches include meditation practices and exercises, for example yoga or T'ai chi, shamanistic practices and traditional medicine. Claxton (1986), Watts (1973), Fromm and Suzuki (1960), Welwood

(1983) and Levine (1979) have discussed this approach. Aspects of this vast field are covered later in this book, under headings such as meditation, shamanism, traditional medicine and yoga.

Kovel (1978) next describes the group approaches such as traditional group therapy, encounter groups, est, psychodrama, transactional analysis; and family therapy. These therapies all developed in the 1960s and 1970s, and work with the group as an agent of change. With the exception of psychodrama, they will not be considered in detail in this book though many alternative therapists use group techniques as a medium for their own special skills and techniques. Readings in this field include works by Bion (1961), Berne (1964) and Harris (1973).

The behavioural directive therapies as defined by Kovel include somatic therapy, sex therapy, directive therapy (hypnotherapy), reality therapy, rational-emotive therapy, and behaviour therapy. In general, these therapies are directive and focused on obtaining particular behaviour changes, and as such do not fit into the range of therapies covered in this book, which rely on personal responsibility, self-direction and expanding awareness at all levels. Apart from hypnotherapy (which is used by many alternative therapists, often in a non-directive manner), they are not therefore considered in the book.

Dryden (1984) provides a useful resource which covers many of the therapies not included in this book: psychodynamic therapies – Freudian, Kleinian, Jungian; personal construct therapy; existential therapy; transactional analysis; rational-emotive therapy; and behavioural therapies.

Kovel's (1978) ideas are useful but now dated as many of the alternative therapies now widely known and used did not exist when his book was written. Examples include physical therapies such as acupressure and Shiatsu (which although ancient in origin are relatively new to the Western world), psychological therapies such as co-counselling (which was developed in the mid-1970s), and neurolinguistic programming (which developed in the 1970s as a result of an investigation into the work of key therapists such as Satir and used ideas from linguistics and computer science), and spiritual therapies such as crystal healing. Many older therapies such as shamanism, some of the tools and techniques of traditional medicine (as practised in parts of Africa, say), and spiritual healing are now beginning to be incorporated into the range of skills and techniques offered by individual therapists. The field is constantly growing, changing and developing. In some ways, an integration is taking place as many individual therapists now offer an individualized synthesis of a range of therapeutic practice. In other ways there is an increasing diversification and specialization of therapeutic skills and techniques.

SOCIAL AND POLITICAL CONNECTIONS

As stated earlier in this chapter, most therapies recognize the importance of and work towards personal responsibility and self-direction. This has implications at social and political levels as anyone who has been involved in personal change is less likely to accept a therapist, employer, organization or government having power over him or her. Ernst and Goodison (1981) begin to explore the links between therapy, social and political realities. An early summary of the applications of humanistic psychology appears in Rowan (1976).

Much of the work in this area has been carried out by the women's movement and in many countries women's therapy centres are available in larger towns. These centres offer therapy based on a developmental model of women which is different from the traditional (often male-dominated) model. The centres use women-based versions of both traditional and alternative therapies. There is a large literature in this area which includes books by Ernst and Goodison (1981), Ernst and Maguire (1987), Eichenbaum and Orbach (1982) and journals such as *Feminist Therapy*.

The development of an alternative women's spirituality movement in the last decade has also been affected by the alternative therapies. Authors such as Mariechild (1981, 1987) have offered a variety of techniques which include meditations and guided visualizations, to enable women to become integrated and whole. These developments are firmly based in the concept of personal empowerment.

Another area where the alternative therapies have had an impact is in the peace movement. The work by Starhawk (1982) clearly makes connections between the inner and outer realities as facilitated by personal growth and change. One effect of changing our inner reality is that our outer reality may no longer be congruent and so there is likely to be a move to change the outer reality. The work of Joanna Macey also links personal empowerment with living in a nuclear age. She draws upon alternative therapy techniques and Buddhist practice as can be seen in her book *Despair and Personal Power in the Nuclear Age* (1983).

In conclusion, the alternative therapies help to promote personal empowerment and wholeness by a variety of different techniques and processes. These changes may take place at an inner level and affect physical, psychological or spiritual processes and patterns, and may then be expressed at an outer level through interpersonal relationships or social and political realities.

REFERENCES

Berne, E. (1964) *Games People Play,* Grove, New York.

Bion, W. R. (1961) *Experience in Groups,* Tavistock, London.

Boadella, D. (1985) *Wilhelm Reich. The Evolution of His Work,* Arkana, London.

Claxton, G. (Ed) (1986) *Beyond Therapy: The Impact of Eastern Religions on Psychological Theory and Practice,* Wisdom, London.

Dryden, W. (1984) *Individual Therapy in Britain,* Harper & Row, London.

Eichenbaum, L. and Orbach, S. (1982) *Outside In. Inside Out. Women's Psychology: A Psychoanalytic Approach,* Penguin, Harmondsworth.

Ernst, S. and Goodison, L. (1981) *In Our Own Hands: A Book of Self-help Therapy,* Women's Press, London.

Ernst, S. and Maguire, M. (Eds) (1987) *Living With the Sphinx: Papers From the Women's Therapy Centre,* Women's Press, London.

Fromm, E. and Suzuki, D. T. (1960) *Zen Buddhism and Psychoanalysis,* Allen & Unwin, London.

Harris, T. (1973) *I'm OK – You're OK,* Pan, London.

Heron, J. (1987) *Confessions of a Janus-brain. A Personal Account of Living in Two Worlds,* Endymion Press, London.

IDHP (Institute for the Development of Human Potential, UK) (1986) *Diploma in humanistic psychology at Leeds,* pamphlet describing the course, Leeds.

Kovel, J. (1978) *A Complete Guide to Therapy,* Penguin, Harmondsworth.

Levine, S. (1979) *A Gradual Awakening,* Century, London.

Macey, J. R. (1983) *Despair and Personal Power in the Nuclear Age,* New Society, Philadelphia.

Mariechild, D. (1981) *Mother Wit. A Feminist Guide to Psychic Development,* Crossing Press, New York.

Mariechild, D. (1987) *The Inner Dance. A Guide to Spiritual and Psychological Unfolding,* Crossing Press, Freedom, CA.

Mindell, A. *Dreambody,* Routledge & Kegan Paul, London.

Milroy, V. (1985) Editorial, *Self and Society,* Vol.13, No.6, November/December.

Rogers, C. (1951) *Client-Centered Therapy: Its Current Practice, Implications and Theory,* Houghton Mifflin, Boston.

Rogers, C. (1961) *On Becoming a Person,* Constable, London.

Rowan, J. (1976) *Ordinary Ecstasy. Humanistic Psychology in Action,* Routledge & Kegan Paul, London.

Rowan, J. (1983) *The Reality Game: A Guide to Humanistic Counselling and Therapy,* Routledge & Kegan Paul, London.

Starhawk, (1982) *Dreaming the Dark,* Beacon Press, Boston.

Watts, A. *Psychotherapy East and West,* Penguin, Harmondsworth.

Welwood, J. (Ed) (1983) *Awakening the Heart. East/West Approaches to Psychotherapy and the Healing Relationship,* Shambhala, Boulder and London.

Wilber, K. (1979) *No Boundary: Eastern and Western Approaches to Personal Growth,* Shambhala, Boulder.

Wilber, K. (1980) *The Atman Project: A Transpersonal View of Human Development,* Theosophical Publishing House, Wheaton.

Wilber, K. (1981) *Up from Eden: A Transpersonal View of Human Evolution,* Routledge & Kegan Paul, London. 1981)

3

Searching for information 1

INTRODUCTION

Knowledge can be simply defined as 'what is known'. It may reside within a person, be written down in a book, pamphlet or magazine, or be presented visually or aurally as a film or music cassette.

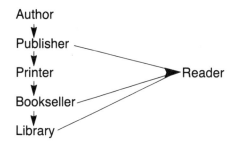

Figure 3.1   The information chain

Knowledge is communicated in a variety of ways – by person-to-person communication, through the so-called information chain (illustrated in Figure 3.1) or by similar chains for other media. This oversimplifies the current situation: authors are also readers and frequently obtain ideas by working with groups of people; musicians may produce and distribute their own recordings. The idea of an 'information chain' is useful when you are searching for information as it suggests points of entry to the required resource. The following sources of information are considered in the first part of this chapter:

Libraries
Bookshops
Publishers.

The second part of this chapter is concerned with the different types of materials which can be found in libraries and bookshops, or obtained from publishers and distributors.

SOURCES OF INFORMATION

Libraries

There are many different kinds of library each with its own purpose, which is reflected in its services and stock.

Public libraries

Public libraries aim to serve the information needs of the local community and operate at two main levels: branch and central.

The branch library is likely to be primarily concerned with lending fiction and non-fiction to adults and children, and providing a small reference collection. Many branch libraries in the UK have small collections of materials on alternative therapy and also some relevant directories. In some public library systems, the branch library does not possess a subject catalogue, which can make searching for information difficult. Many branch libraries maintain registers of local societies and activities and these can be a useful source of information. Similarly, their notice boards may contain news and information about activities in alternative therapy in that area.

The central library provides reference information services, as well as a lending service. These are important sources of information as they frequently hold reference materials which are expensive and unlikely to be found elsewhere. Like the branch library, central libraries frequently maintain registers of local societies and activities.

Academic libraries

These are libraries attached to educational organizations – further education colleges, polytechnics and universities. Their stock and services will reflect the courses taught in the institution and, if these include psychology, social work, or health and related studies, the library stock is likely to include items relevant to people searching for information on alternative therapy. Most academic libraries have good collections of reference books, abstracting and indexing journals and also periodicals. These libraries are generally open to the public for reference purposes.

Special libraries

These are libraries which may cover a particular subject or be attached to a particular organization. Their availability will depend on their purpose. For example, many private companies have special libraries which are open only to their employees, and many specialist societies and associations have libraries which are open to anyone. An example of the latter is found in the Institute of Complementary Medicine in London.

Using a library

Most larger libraries provide printed guides (either to the whole library or to a particular section of it) and signposting to their services.

The process of searching for information in a library is quite simple. If you know the bibliographic details of the item you want, look it up in the author/title catalogue or, for a periodical, in the periodicals catalogue, find the library location mark for the item and then check the shelf. If you cannot find what you require the library staff will help.

If you don't know of any relevant items you will have to carry out a subject search by looking up the subject index and/or classified catalogue(s) held in the library. Identify the classification code(s) of the subject and then check the classified catalogue to identify specific items. Finally check the shelf. This process can be quite time-consuming but if you omit steps and, for example, move straight from subject index to shelf, you are likely to miss items stored at special locations or out on loan. Again, if you have problems or need help ask the librarian.

Bookshops

There are two main kinds of bookshops – traditional and alternative. Increasingly, traditional bookshops are stocking books on the alternative therapies but their stock tends to be restricted to items from key publishers in this field.

Alternative bookshops vary in their subject coverage and range of stock. Shops which specialize in personal growth, health and healing are likely to sell both traditional and alternative publications. They may well sell items which are difficult to obtain from other sources, and also radical journals and magazines.

Publishers

When the library and bookshops are unable to satisfy your information needs you may have to go directly to the publisher. Publishers can be identified through conventional sources, such as *Books in Print* and also *British Books in Print*, which have publisher listings complete with addresses and telephone numbers. However, many alternative therapy publications and their publishers do not appear in these sources. Fortunately, directories exist which can be used to track them down.

TYPES OF MATERIAL

There are three main kinds of material which are likely to answer a person's information requirements: printed materials, audiovisual resources and computerized resources. Each of these materials is briefly described below, their use in searching for information is described in Chapter 4 and specific examples are given in Chapters 5 to 8.

Printed materials

Reference items are used to provide factual information such as names and addresses, and information about books which will enable them to be identified (bibliographic information). Examples covered in this book include:

1 Guides to finding out about libraries, bookshops and publishers.
2 Literature guides – such as this book, which help the reader to find information on a particular topic or in a particular format (such as audiovisual materials).
3 Dictionaries – there are many specialist dictionaries which can be very useful to people searching for definitions and so on in the field of alternative therapy.
4 Encyclopedias – both general and specialist encyclopedias are useful sources of historical and sometimes more up-to-date information.
5 Directories – these are books which contain lists of names and addresses, products or courses. Thousands of directories are published each year and Chapter 5 gives guidance on tracking down a particular directory. This is followed by descriptions and tips on using some important directories relevant to this field.
6 Bibliographies – these are listings of information sources relevant to a particular field or type of material or produced by a particular publisher. Chapter 5 describes tools which can be used for tracking down particular bibliographies and identifies key bibliographies on alternative therapy.

Abstracting and indexing journals are publications which provide detailed information on the contents of periodicals, serials or magazines. This guidance is generally provided by a series of indexes, for example author and subject, to the contents of individual issues of periodicals.

Abstracting journals also include a brief abstract or summary of the articles which have been indexed. Use of these journals saves much time when searching for information in periodicals. Abstracting and indexing journals are frequently three or more months behind published journals, and current awareness journals

27

can be used to cover this time-lag. Chapter 4 provides guidance on using these tools and Chapter 5 gives specific examples.

Periodicals – primary journals, serials or magazines – contain articles on specific topics and may contain descriptions of new therapeutic techniques, advertisements for workshops and individual practices, book reviews and bibliographies. Some are published by academic publishers and may be abstracted and indexed in the sources mentioned above. Others may be published by co-operatives, networks or individuals and be prepared on typewriters or home computers and photocopied for circulation. These alternative publications can be quite hard to track down and they may have a short life span. Chapter 5 looks at sources of information on identifying and locating both traditional and alternative periodicals. Specific examples of periodicals on different alternative therapies are given in Chapters 6, 7 and 8.

Books or monographs may contain details of an author's own ideas or experiences, summaries of ideas, theories, or collections of papers by a number of people. They can be identified using bibliographies (which may be issued by national libraries, associations, bookshops or publishers) or library catalogues. Bibliographies are described in detail in Chapter 5 and many of the resources cited in Chapters 5 to 9 are books.

Pamphlets are printed publications which may vary in size (A4 and smaller) and number of pages. They are frequently published by individuals and associations and can be quite difficult to trace. They often contain information not available elsewhere. They are not considered in any detail in this work.

Official publications frequently contain documentary evidence to support the work carried out for governments, non-government bodies (such as the World Health Organization), and other organizations. Some official publications are relevant to the field of alternative therapy. An example of this kind of report is the British Medical Association's evaluation of alternative medicine which include a number of alternative therapies. Information sources on official publications are considered in Chapter 5.

Research publications contain detailed information about research projects: literature surveys and state-of-the-art reports; methodologies, results; discussions and conclusions; and bibliographies. They may be published as theses or dissertations, and methods of identifying and locating these sources are described in Chapter 5. They may also be published as periodical articles or reports (see above). Methods of identifying current research in progress are also described in Chapter 5.

Audiovisual resources

General information sources concerned with identifying and locating audiovisual resources are covered in Chapter 5, while sources related to a particular type of therapy are located under the relevant subject heading in Chapters 6 to 8. Audiovisual resources can be divided into two main groups.

Film and video which are becoming increasingly important in the world of alternative therapy, particularly in the areas of education and training.

Cassettes and, to a lesser extent, *records* are widely used by therapists who may use commercially available cassettes or specialized, 'home-produced' tapes. Cassettes used may range from classical or electronic music, relaxation and meditation music, to natural sounds such as whale noises.

Computerized resources

Computerized sources are becoming increasingly important to alternative therapists. They can be divided into three groups:

On-line databases
CD-ROM
Videotex.

On-line databases – it is possible to carry out an information search which involves accessing files held on a computer. Most main libraries offer on-line computer search services (for which they may charge) and provided you have the appropriate equipment, software and permission it is possible to carry out these searches on a home computer. On-line searching is a relatively cheap method of searching large computer files which may contain details of periodical articles, association names and addresses and books. The advantages and disadvantages of on-line searching and the process involved are described in detail in Chapter 4 and useful on-line databases are described in Chapter 5.

CD-ROM is a relatively new format and is of interest here as increasingly the files and databases available from the on-line search services are becoming available on CD-ROM and so access to this information is cheaper. The initials CD-ROM stand for compact disc–read only memory, and it is now possible to buy CD-ROM drives for microcomputers in the same way as compact disc players for hi-fi units.

Videotex is a term used to describe two main types of computerized information systems: viewdata systems such as PRESTEL; and teletext systems such as ORACLE. The difference between these two systems and their relevance to the alternative therapies are considered in Chapters 4 and 5.

4

Searching for information   2

Searching for information can be a time-consuming and expensive process. In this chapter, we look at:

The search strategy
Contacting people or organizations
The manual search – using abstracting and indexing journals
Computerized searches.

THE SEARCH STRATEGY

The search strategy described here can be used by people searching for different kinds of information and it will help the searcher find the required information in the most effective manner.

The detailed search strategy is summarized in Figure 4.1 and expanded in the following sections. It is possible to omit some of the steps in this process, for example a practitioner may not need to check search terms in dictionaries and so on. However, care should be taken if steps are omitted as it can lead to an incomplete search and missed information.

Starting the search

Equip yourself with paper: 5 x 3 inch (12.5 x 7.5 cm) record cards are particularly useful if you are searching for journal or book references which you may want to rearrange at a later date; or a notebook if you are seeking a few items of information. It is

Information source	Process
	START
Dictionary, encyclopedia ————	Identify the search topic
Directories ————————	Are you looking for information
No	from people or organizations?
		Yes
Computerized search ————	Is the search suitable for a manual
No	literature search?
		Yes
Literature guides ————————	Identify the sources
Directories ————————	Is it a simple enquiry requiring a
Yes	factual answer?
		No
Library catalogues ————————	Are you looking for a book,
Bibliographies Yes	audiovisual material or a
	multimedia item?
		No
Abstracting and indexing ————	Are you looking for periodical
journals Yes	articles on your topic?
On-line sources	
		No
Current awareness tools, ————	Do you want to update your
current journals Yes	search?
		No
Librarian ————————	Have you found the answer to your
Information scientist No	enquiry?
		Yes
	FINISH

Figure 4.1   Searching for information

important to keep detailed notes of where you search, the search terms used and any references that you find, as this information will enable you to track down items and extend your search without having to do any extra work. The minimum amount of information needed for a book reference is:

Title
Author
Place of publication, publisher, date

and for a journal article:

Article title
Author
Journal title
Volume, issue, year, pagination.

If the book or journal looks very obscure then it is also worthwhile noting down the publisher's address and the ISBN or ISSN (the International Standard Book/Serial Number).

Identify the scope of the subject

Define your subject and identify possible search terms and their synonyms. Use dictionaries, encyclopedias, glossaries (often found in the back of books), thesauri, or key books on the subject. It is worthwhile noting any different spellings or word usages, for example between American and British terminology.

Identify the scope of the enquiry

What is the time scope of your search – do you want to find everything published in the last six months or sixteen years? Do you want to restrict your search to English language materials? Do you want to find all different types of materials (printed, media, or computer-based) or only one type of material? Do you want to identify people and organizations? If so, do you want to restrict the search to people and organizations in one country? How much time are you willing to put into the search? What library and other facilities are you willing to use? Are you willing to pay for inter-library loans?

Analyse the subject of your search

Identify different aspects of your search. To give an example, a search on astrology and therapy may be broken down into the applications of natal astrology and gestalt therapy in group therapy.

Consider the literature of each aspect. In this example, group therapy is likely *not* to be concerned with group therapy in traditional education, health and social service situations, so it *may* be possible to omit the literatures of these subjects from the search.

Identify all likely subject headings. It is worth identifying broader subject headings which contain the required subject, narrower subjects which contain the subjects sought, and also related subjects. For example, the broader term *recreation therapy* includes the narrower term *music therapy*, which is the focus of the search.

Starting the search

Once you have defined the scope of your subject and enquiry you will need to decide whether or not you can find the information you are seeking by:

Contacting people or organizations
A manual literature search
A computerized search.

These different types of search are described in detail later in this chapter.

Obtaining specific items

Once you have identified particular items that look as if they are relevant to your needs you will then need to obtain a copy of them. If you have tracked down an item in the library you will be able to borrow it if you are a member of the library (unless it is labelled for reference only). Even if you are not a member you will probably be able to use it in the library and perhaps photocopy relevant sections. If the item is not held in your library you could ask the library staff to check local union catalogues (catalogues of library holdings for a number of libraries in a particular region) to see if it is held in another library in your area. If not, ask the library to borrow the item for you on the inter-library loan system. The librarian will then borrow the item from another library (either in the same or a different country). This service can take a few weeks and you may be charged for it.

Many libraries do not stock items on alternative therapy and so you may have to obtain the materials you need from a bookshop. Many specialist bookshops in alternative therapy also provide very good mail order services so that you do not need to visit them. Finally, if the bookshops are unable to help you may be able to obtain the item you need by contacting the publisher direct.

Selecting appropriate materials

Once you have identified and obtained specific items it is important to check their quality. The following criteria can be used to evaluate materials.

Check the subject coverage in the item. Is it very narrow or broad? Is it comprehensive or are key topics omitted? In what way is it biased? Is the level appropriate to your needs?

Is the item indexed? Does it contain a bibliography? If it does, then is the bibliography up to date? Are any key items known to you omitted from the bibliography? Is the bibliography biased towards publications from a particular author, country or publisher?

What do you know of the author? His or her experience and qualifications? Is the author trying to sell a process or product?

Ending your search

Once you have found items that suit your needs you will have come to the end of your search. I always find it useful to keep the records and findings of any information search I make as I often find that I make a similar search in the near future or someone comes and asks me for information on the same or a related topic.

CONTACTING PEOPLE OR ORGANIZATIONS

Information is often available only from a particular person or organization. Frequently organizations have prepared booklists and bibliographies, directories, and registers of practitioners which may save you a considerable amount of time. Chapter 9 describes some of the organizations and societies involved in alternative therapy and shows you how to find out about organizations and individuals. It is divided into the following sections:

People, for example practitioners, trainers, authors
Informal groups and networks
Societies and associations
Current activities.

MANUAL LITERATURE SEARCHES

A manual literature search is probably one of the most common types of information searches and it involves using catalogues and indexes to identify and locate items which contain relevant information. This type of search is normally carried out in libraries and, perhaps, bookshops.

The main stages involved in a manual literature search are described in Figure 4.1 The different kinds of materials which may be used when carrying out an extensive literature search are outlined in Chapter 3. In this section, we look at using abstracting and indexing journals. Specific examples are listed in the relevant section in Chapters 5 to 8.

Using abstracting and indexing journals

Abstracting and indexing journals were described in Chapter 3, as were periodicals. In this section, we look at their use in the search.

Thousands of periodicals are published each year and many of them contain articles about alternative therapy. These articles may be found in alternative periodicals or in traditional periodicals in the fields of education, medicine, psychology, religion or social sciences. It would be an impossible task for anyone to read all of them. However, abstracting and indexing journals exist to enable the information searcher to identify relevant articles.

Many journals contain references to articles on alternative therapy, and these are described in Chapter 5. In this section, we look at:

General guidelines for using abstracting and indexing services
Using *Psychological Abstracts*
Using *Index Medicus*.

General guidelines for using abstracting and indexing journals

Identify the indexes to the abstracting and indexing journal. Is there an author index? Is there a subject index? Are the indexes cumulated?

Read the instructions for using the index(es). Is there a vocabulary control system, such as a thesaurus, which specifies which terms are index terms? If a thesaurus or classification system is used, how are changes and updates introduced into the system? What filing rules are followed – letter by letter or word by word? What are the rules with respect to use of British or American spellings? How are abbreviations handled?

Normally you begin searching in the most recent issue available and search backwards in time. Note down the volume and issue numbers of the abstracting and indexing journals searched, the search terms used and record any relevant references. Look out for changes in indexing policies.

If you do not find any relevant articles broaden your search. Check that you are searching under appropriate search terms for that particular abstracting journal.

Using *Psychological Abstracts*

Psychological Abstracts has been published since its origination in 1926 by the American Psychological Association (APA). It covers the contents of over 1200 journals concerned with psychology or related fields. The bias is towards US publications and English language materials. It is published monthly and abstracts are arranged in general subject order under the headings listed in the contents page. These headings can be used to identify the section most relevant to the user's general needs and to help browsing. Headings include Parapsychology, Learning and memory, Psychosexual behavior and sex roles.

For subject searches, the user needs to refer to the *Thesaurus of Psychological Terms* (4th edn, 1985), published by The APA,

Washington, DC, which provides guidance on terms which can be used for searching *Psychological Abstracts*. It is divided into sections, with an introduction, a relationships section and a rotated alphabetical terms section.

For example, someone searching for items on dream therapy will find no entry in the thesaurus (in the relationships section) for that phrase. However, an entry does exist for dream analysis:

Dream analysis
PN 302
    UF Dream interpretation
    B   Psychoanalysis
            Psychoanalysis therapeutic techniques
            Psychotherapy
    R   Analysis/
            Parapsychology

The abbreviations used for the entries have the following meanings:

SC *Subject code* – a unique five-digit subject code which can be used for on-line searches
UF *Use for* – indicates terms which are not used as index terms or entry points
B *Broader term* – keywords which have a broader meaning and can be used to broaden the scope of a search
R *Related term* – keywords on themes which may also be of interest to the searcher.

Other abbreviations include:

PN *Posting note* – a note for on-line searchers which indicates the number of abstracts indexed to date with this term
N *Narrower term* – which indicates keywords which are more specific than the preferred term and can be used to narrow a search
Use – guides the user from a keyword which is not used as an index term to one that is
SN *Scope note* – provides additional information to guide the user as to the meaning or usage of the keyword.

The rotated alphabetical terms section is a permutated subject index in which every part of a phrase has an entry point in the appropriate alphabetical section. So, dream analysis can be found under both dream and analysis. This part of the thesaurus is useful for identifying related keywords which can then be checked in the relationships section.

Items are indexed under the preferred term given in the thesaurus in the brief subject index in each monthly volume. Searchers for information on alternative therapy will find that only well-established therapies such as music therapy have their own entry point in the thesaurus. Other therapies such as co-counselling and Reichian therapy do not occur and searchers must therefore carry out lengthy manual or on-line searches to find appropriate references.

In the brief subject index each keyword is followed by one or more abstract numbers and the user must then turn to the main section of the volume and find the abstract. After reading the abstract, it is possible to decide whether or not the original item is worth obtaining. The brief subject index also contains some of the guiding found in the thesaurus and users are directed from disallowed terms to preferred terms.

Each monthly issue also contains an author index which is a fairly straightforward alphabetical listing. Possible points of confusion are made clear in the introduction to the index.

Until January 1986 quarterly cumulative indexes were produced for *Psychological Abstracts* but since then monthly and annual indexes only have been produced. The cumulative indexes make retrospective searching much easier. They are organized in the same way as the monthly issues.

Using *Index Medicus*

Index Medicus has been published since 1879 and covers medical and related fields. It is produced as a result of indexing over 2500 journals and over 70 per cent of the items covered are in English.

To use *Index Medicus* it is necessary to become familiar with a number of tools which are provided to facilitate its use.

Public MeSH is a thesaurus which can be used to identify preferred and non-preferred terms. It contains much useful information: details of indexing policies and changes of policy for particular terms; relationships between terms (similar to those used in *Psycho-*

logical Abstracts but with different abbreviations); keyword code numbers which are needed for use of the *Tree structures*.

Annotated MeSH is similar to *Public MeSH* but provides additional information and is of particular relevance to on-line searchers.

Tree structures provides a semantically related tree of terms. The 16 000 terms in MeSH are assigned to one or more broad headings and are then placed in a hierarchical arrangement. The keyword codes mentioned above are tree codes and relate to the position of a term in a hierarchy. They can be used for on-line searching.

Permuted MeSH is a rotated subject index which can be used to find the entry point or preferred order of keywords in a phrase for use in the thesaurus.

Another tool, of little interest to people searching for information on alternative therapy, is *MeSH Supplementary Chemical Records*.
   Detailed guidance on using these tools is included in their introductions and also in *How to Use Index Medicus and Excerpta Medica* by Barry Strickland-Hodge (1986, Gower, Aldershot).

Index Medicus is published monthly and *MeSH* is distributed with the January Part 2 issue. Entries are arranged in the main volume under subject terms as defined by *MeSH*. There is also an author section.

COMPUTERIZED SEARCHES

There are three main types of computer search likely to be of interest to anyone searching for information on alternative therapy. The first involves searching on-line databases owned by host suppliers (in this book referred to as 'on-line searching'), while the second involves searching CD-ROM versions of these databases. Finally, there is the search of specialized on-line systems called videotex. These different methods of accessing computer-held information will be dealt with in turn.

On-line searching

On-line searching involves accessing computer-held files which may contain bibliographic records. These files are frequently held on what is called a 'host' computer system and by accessing one host it is possible to gain access to many different files from many different sources. The host system can be accessed via the telephone and telecommunications systems, and so it is possible to access computer-held files in different countries.

The advantages of on-line searching include fast access to a wide range of information sources; fast and accurate searching as compared with manual searches; very detailed searches being possible; access to very up-to-date information; and access to information which may not be otherwise available. The disadvantages of on-line searching include the cost; the need for the user to be specially trained; the fact that the databases tend to cover materials published since the early 1970s and so cannot be used for materials published earlier.

Most main and specialized libraries offer on-line search services and have specially trained staff who will be able to help the user decide whether or not an on-line search is an appropriate method of obtaining the required information.

Most on-line systems are made up of the following components:

Information sources
Computer hardware
Telecommunications systems
Computer software.

Information sources

These may be the computer-based version of printed products such as abstracting and indexing journals (for example *Index Medicus* and *Psychological Abstracts*) or directories (for example *Directory of Associations*), or may be special files which do not have a printed equivalent. This situation is summarized in Figure 4.2.

The information is stored in the computer in records, and different database producers have different record structures. Most records contain the following information:

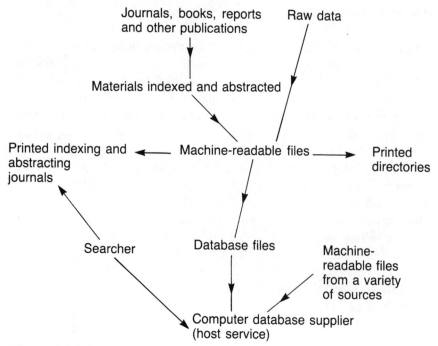

Figure 4.2   Computerized information sources

Record number
Title of article
Author(s)
Title of journal
Volume, issue, date, pagination
Language
Subject descriptors
Special indexing codes
Abstract.

Figure 4.3 shows a typical record from the Medline training file. Most records are stored in a file in record number order, with the most recent record first, and special indexes are created in additional files called index files. These enable fast and specific searches to be carried out.

(Note the abstract has been omitted)

AN 86084770
AU Kornfield-A-D
TI Hypnosis and behaviour therapy II: Contemporary developments.
SO Int-J-Psychosom 1985, VOL: 32 (4), P: 13-7 33 Refs.
LG EN.
DE Anxiety Disorders/therapy;
   Behaviour Therapy/* ;
   Cognition;
   Combined Modality Therapy;
   Conditioning, Operant;
   Desensitization (Psychology);
   Human;
   Hypnosis/* ;
   Imagination;
   Implosive therapy;
   Psychotherapy, Rational-Emotive;
   Relaxation Technics;
   Review.
YR 85.
ZN ZI-107-567-875
JC GTC.
IM 8604
ED 860219.

Figure 4.3   Typical record from the Medline training file

Computer hardware

The hardware or equipment needed for on-line searching is illustrated in Figure 4.4. It generally consists of:

Computer terminal
Printer
Telephone
Modem
Telecommunications network
Host computer.

There are a number of different kinds of terminal which can be
used for on-line searching: a keyboard combined with a visual
display unit (VDU); a teletypewriter (combined keyboard and

43

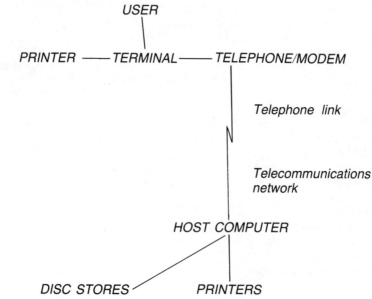

Figure 4.4   Computer hardware used for on-line searching

printer); an intelligent terminal (keyboard combined with a VDU with some processing power and memory); a microcomputer (keyboard, VDU, central processing unit and external storage units). Increasingly, people are using microcomputers as terminals for on-line searching.

If you carry out an on-line search with a printer attached to your terminal you will be able to keep a hard copy of the search, and to have the results of an urgent search printed out immediately (though this is more expensive than having a printout sent to you through the post).

The computer terminal can be connected to the host computer system via a telephone and telecommunications network. The purpose of the piece of equipment called the modem is to translate the signals from the computer into a form in which they can be sent along the telecommunications systems.

Ideally the telephone used for on-line searching should be a direct line and not go via a switchboard where the line may accidentally be cut off or internal calls may cut off transmission. If a great deal of on-line searching is to be carried out it is worthwhile reserving a special telephone for on-line use and keeping its number private.

The main on-line hosts are used by thousands of searchers daily and the host computer system is likely to be a series of mainframe computers with many peripherals (printers, disc storage and VDUs). There are a number of these systems, including DIALOG (USA) and DATASTAR (Switzerland).

Telecommunications network

Rather than pay for the cost of long-distance telephone calls, it is cheaper and more efficient to use international telecommunications networks to access the host computer systems. These networks are designed for transmitting information to and from computers and examples include Tymnet, Telenet and IPSS (British Telecom's International Package Switching Service). Access to these networks can be via national telecommunications systems (in the UK British Telecom), which charge for the amount of time used (this is called the connect time).

Computer software

The host computer systems have their own software, which is used for housekeeping purposes and is also the means by which the user can access, search and manipulate the information held on the computer. The user must learn the characteristics of the host computer's command language or user access software.

If you use a microcomputer as a terminal for on-line searching you will need special telecommunications software to enable the microcomputer to act as a terminal and communicate with the host system. This software will carry out the following functions:

1 Set the protocol (the parameters or settings by which the two computers will communicate).
2 Create a memory space or buffer in the microcomputer's central processing unit.
3 Display on the screen what is being typed on the keyboard or sent from the host computer.
4 Enable incoming and outgoing information to be stored to and from the external memory units (discs or tapes).

5 Send and receive information to and from the modem.
6 Control the printer.

More specialized software will also provide:

7 Automatic log-on, using stored telecommunications network identifiers and passwords and host computer identifiers and passwords, which can then be transmitted by pressing a few keys.
8 Store and forward searches which enable search strategies to be typed in off-line, errors corrected and then forwarded on-line to the host computer system. This can save expensive on-line time otherwise spent in the possibly slow typing and correction of errors.
9 Downloading which is obtaining information (for example records from a host computer) and storing it on the storage devices (discs) of your own microcomputer.
10 Searching aids such as the automatic storage of command languages and the translation of searches from one host's command language to another.

Carrying out an on-line search

Preparing for an on-line search generally takes up much more time than the actual search. A number of questions need to be answered:

1 Will the on-line search provide the appropriate information?
2 Is it the most appropriate source of information?
3 Is it a cost-effective means of obtaining this information?
4 Which databases need to be searched? (Take into account: subject and journal coverage; record coverage indexing methods; up-to-dateness; costs and accessibility. If a comprehensive search is required a large collection of databases may need to be searched.)
5 Which host system needs to be used? (Take into account: subjects and databases covered by the host; search facilities, including sophisticated searching devices; print facilities; cost of the host system.)

The next step is to work out your on-line strategy, which initially involves analysing the search topic and breaking it down into its logical components. For example:

Topic
Use of gestalt techniques in astrological counselling. Articles published in English after 1982.

Breakdown
Gestalt
Astrological counselling
English language
1982 onwards.

The next step is to select search terms with the aid of dictionaries, thesauri, glossaries, classification schemes, textbooks and on-line vocabulary tools. For example:

Gestalt
Gestalt therapy
Astrology
Astrological counselling
Natal astrology
English language
1982 onwards.

The search terms then need to be put into a format suitable for on-line searching.

1 Check to see how the system and files handle punctuation and word forms. In the example above counselling is spelt with one 'l' in US systems and files and with two in UK systems and files.

2 Check the indexing policies of the system. In the example above the searcher would need to know that some systems have the phrase gestalt therapy as an indexing term while others use 'gestalt, therapy'.

3 Check which fields can be searched. For example, title, descriptors (keywords) or abstract.

4 Check methods of limiting the search. In the example above the search needs to be limited by language and date.

5 Check for and remove potentially high-posted, general terms such as therapy, education.

6 Check for proximity searching tools. In the example above there

is a need to search for the phrases 'astrological counselling' and 'natal astrology'. In some systems this can be done by using the command (w), which means 'with' and the phrases would be typed in in the following format: astrological(w)counselling and natal(w)astrology.

The search (as it will be typed into the terminal) can now be planned in detail. This involves:

1 Finding the system commands. These can be obtained from the system manual and command summaries. The system commands will enable the searcher to enter a particular database or file, search it, display the results of the search on the VDU screen, print out the results of the search, leave the system.
2 Organizing the search terms obtained from the procedure described above using the Boolean operators AND, OR and NOT, as indicated in Figure 4.5. At this stage it is worthwhile planning what to do if the search is too broad (and, say, throws up thousands of references) or too narrow, and to draw up contingency plans.

The on-line search can now be carried out. This will involve connecting to a telecommunications network, accessing and entering a host system, entering a particular database or file and searching it, displaying the results of the search on the VDU screen and printing them out, and leaving the file and the system. An example of a search is given in Figure 4.6.

Searching CD-ROM

There are now an increasing number of on-line databases available in CD-ROM (Compact Disc–Read Only Memory) format which is a product of laser technology. CD-ROM discs are similar to audio compact discs but they can store 600Mb (600 000 000 letters, punctuation marks or numbers) or more of digitally encoded information.

CD-ROM can be searched with the aid of IBM PC or compatible microcomputers with a CD-ROM disc drive.

AND is used to narrow a search.

Set 1 Set 2
Gestalt   Astrology

Set 1 AND Set 2 is equivalent to the shaded area and contains references on gestalt *and* astrology.

OR is used to broaden a search.

Set 1 Set 2
Gestalt   Astrology

Set 1 OR Set 2 is equivalent to the shaded area and contains references on either gestalt, astrology *or* both.

NOT is used to exclude a topic from the search.

Set 1 Set 2
Gestalt   Astrology

Set 1 NOT Set 2 is equivalent to the shaded area and contains references on Gestalt but *not* on Astrology. In this case, items on Gestalt *and* Astrology are excluded from the selected set of references.

Figure 4.5   Boolean operators

Searching CD-ROM can often be carried out at different levels. Whitaker's *Bookbank* CD-ROM service can be searched at novice, intermediate and expert levels. Novice and intermediate levels involve the use of menus, while expert is command-driven and offers the level and sophistication of commands found with on-line host systems. Search responses can be displayed and printed out to user-defined formats.

Searching videotex

Videotex is a term used to describe information systems which display screens full of data sequentially in a set format, which in the UK uses colour and graphics with a maximum of 960 characters per screen. The screen can be a television screen or a computer's VDU. Two types of videotex are available.

```
LEE/A01-5326540029
NDIALOG
ADD?
A212300120

23412300120+COM

ENTER YOUR DIALOG PASSWORD
@@@@@@@ LOGON File1 Tue 12 Jan 87 5:39:45 Port06E
** FILE 61 LIMITS ARE NOT WORKING **
? BEGIN 154
      12 Jan87 5:40:40 User 1234
   $0.30 0.017 Hrs File1*

File 154: MEDLINE – 80-87/Jan
   Set  Items    Descriptions
? SELECT GESTALT
   1    143      Gestalt
? SELECT ASTROLOGY
   2    3        Astrology
? Combine 1 and 2
   3    0        1 AND 2
? PRINT 1/5/1-3
```

Figure 4.6   Example of an on-line search

Teletext – non-interactive videotex which is broadcast by the television service. Examples include CEEFAX and ORACLE. The amount of information stored on teletext is limited and so it is unlikely to contain any detailed information of relevance to people searching for information on the alternative therapies.

Viewdata – interactive videotex which is characterized by the need for a telephone to access an external computerized database. Examples include Minitel, Prestel and booking systems used by many travel agents. The amount of information stored on viewdata systems is limited only by the size of the computer storage system and the policies of the owners of the system. Some systems, such as Prestel, do contain some information on the alternative therapies and related organizations. This information can easily be accessed using the menu-driven system. Many public libraries in the UK possess Prestel sets which can be used for on-line searching.

PART II

THE INFORMATION SOURCES: A BIBLIOGRAPHY

5

General information sources

General information sources are those which cover a wide number of subjects including the alternative therapies. Sources relating to specific therapies are looked at in Chapters 6 to 8. This chapter is divided into

Printed sources
Audiovisual resources
Computerized sources.

PRINTED SOURCES

This section deals with:

Reference items
   Guides to libraries, bookshops and publishers
   Literature guides
   Dictionaries
   Encyclopedias
   Directories
   Bibliographies
Abstracting and indexing journals
Periodicals
Official publications
Research publications.

Reference items

Guides to libraries

The following guides can be used to track down libraries with special collections in your field of interest:

American Library Directory, 38th edn. Edited by Jaques Cattell Press (New York: Bowker, 1985).
This is in two volumes. The arrangement is geographic and individual entries are detailed.

ASLIB Directory. Volume 2: Information Sources in Medicine, the Social Sciences and the Humanities, 5th edn. Edited by Ellen M. Codlin (London: ASLIB, 1984).
See section on Directories.

Directory of Medical and Health Care Libraries. Edited by W. D. Linton (London: LA, 1987).
This directory includes some libraries which hold items on the alternative therapies. It is a well-produced publication with good indexes.

Directory of Special Libraries and Information Centres, 8th edn. Edited by B. T. Darnay (Detroit: Gale, 1983).
In three volumes, this publication has over 16 000 detailed entries with a variety of subject indexes.

Encyclopedia of Information Systems and Services (Detroit: Gale, 1987).
This book gives detailed descriptions of more than 3500 organizations in the USA and other countries that either produce or provide access to computerized information in all subject areas.

Libraries in the United Kingdom and the Republic of Ireland, 11th edn. (London: Library Association, 1985).
This directory covers public, university, polytechnic and selected other libraries.

Subject Collections in European Libraries, 2nd edn. By R. C. Lewanski (New York: Bowker, 1978).
Libraries are arranged according to subject specialism (following

the 18th edition of the Dewey Decimal Classification scheme) and there is a subject index. Coverage is especially comprehensive of the UK, Scandinavia, the Low Countries and Germany.

World Guide to Libraries, 6th edn. Edited by H. Lengenfelder (Munich: Saur, 1983; Detroit: Gale, 1983).
This directory lists approximately 40 000 libraries in 167 countries. The arrangement is A-Z by country within broad continental regions, and coverage includes all kinds of libraries.

World Guide to Special Libraries, 1st edn. Edited by H. Lengenfelder (Munich: Saur, 1983; Detroit: Gale, 1983).
This directory lists approximately 32 000 libraries in 159 countries. The arrangement is by subject, and headings include social sciences, health and life sciences. Within each subject the arrangement is A–Z by country. The entries are detailed and future editions are likely to cover additional libraries.

Guides to bookshops

In the UK traditional bookshops can be found using the *Yellow Pages* telephone directory. Alternative bookshops can be tracked down through the organization Radical Bookseller (265 Seven Sisters Road, London N4 2DE) which publishes a journal of the same title. The *Radical Bookseller* contains news of the alternative press and booksellers and at regular intervals contains a detailed listing of 'Radical bookshops in Britain and Ireland'. This lists bookshops according to geographic location and each entry contains the following information:

Name, address, telephone number
Opening hours
Specialist subjects
Services
Booklists available.

There is also a shop name index.
  The bookshops which I have found most useful and which have decent stocks of overseas materials are:

Changes Bookshop
242 Belsize Road, London NW6 4BT
01–328 5161
This shop maintains a large collection of alternative therapy materials, it has a mail order service and produces helpful booklists, for example *A Catalogue of Books on Neurolinguistic Programming* and *A Catalogue of Books on Ericksonian Approaches to Hypnosis and Psychotherapy*.

Compendium Books
243 Camden High Street, London NW1 8QS
01–485 8944
This shop maintains a good collection of alternative therapy materials and also covers other subjects such as politics and feminism. It has a mail order service and produces booklists, a recent example being *Therapy and Creativity*.

In other countries, bookshops can be tracked down using similar tools, such as telephone directories, and association or alternative directories. A useful source which tries to cover the world is:

A Pilgrim's Guide to Planet Earth. Edited by Parmatma Singh Khalsa (San Rafael, California: Spiritual Community Publications, 1981).
This book covers the world and the entries are divided under geographical headings: West Europe; Scandinavia; East Europe; North Africa; Sub-Sahara Africa; Middle East; Route to India; East Asia; the Pacific; Latin America; and North America. The North America section is divided into Canada and the United States, and the latter is divided by state, then by city or place name, and entries are classified into: ashram; bookstore; centre; foodstore; monastery; restaurant; school; and other. While this directory is not comprehensive it provides an excellent starting place.

In the USA additional information sources include:

NAM LISTS
PO Box 1067SB, Berkeley, CA 94701
(415) 644–3299
This is a computerized mailing list service which covers bookstores, mail order suppliers, and periodicals.

The New Consciousness Sourcebook. By Parmatma Singh Khalsa (Pomona, CA: Arcline, 1985).
This publication contains a number of bookstores and book distributors in its classified listings.

Guides to publishers

Publishers can be tracked down through conventional sources, such as *Books in Print* and also *British Books in Print* (see Bibliographies), which have publisher listings complete with their addresses and telephone numbers. However, many alternative therapy publications and their publishers do not reach these sources. Fortunately directories exist which can be used to track them down:

Alternatives in Print: An International Catalogue of Books, Pamphlets, Periodicals and Audiovisual Materials. Compiled by the Task Force on Alternatives in Print, Social Responsibilities Round Table, ALA (New York: Neal-Schuman, 1980). Available in the UK from Mansell.
American Publishers and Their Addresses. By R. Shepherd (Beckenham: Trigon Press, 1982).
Directory of Book Publishers and Wholesalers with Their Terms and Agents for Overseas Publishers (London: Booksellers Association). Annual.
Hard-to-Find Publishers and Their Addresses (London: Alan Armstrong, 1987).
This book was previously published as *5001 Hard-to-Find Publishers and Their Addresses* and it now lists more than 7500 entries, listed alphabetically by name, and each entry includes the name, address, telephone, telex, telefax and distributor. While its coverage is international in scope, it specializes in publishers who produce English language materials.

International Directory of Little Magazines and Small Presses. Edited by Len Fulton (Paradise, CA: Dustbooks, 1985).
Oxbridge Directory of Newsletters. Edited by Patricia Hagood (New York: Oxbridge Communications, 1986).
Publishers in the UK and Their Addresses. (London: Whitaker). Annual.

Small Press Record of Books in Print (Paradise, CA: Dustbooks, 1971–) .
This directory can be used to track down publishers and their addresses, as well as books which are in print.

Standard Periodical Directory. Edited by Patricia Hagood (New York: Oxbridge Communications, 1985).
See section on 'Periodicals'.

Ulrich's International Periodicals Directory (Ann Arbor: Bowker). Biannual.
See section on 'Periodicals'.

Whole Again Resource Guide, 1986/87 edn. By Tim Ryan, Patricia J. Case and others (Santa Barbara, CA: SourceNet, 1986).
See section on 'Directories'.

Literature guides

This book is a literature guide, that is, it aims to assist the reader with the information sources on a particular topic – in this case alternative therapy. Guides to the literature are particularly useful for those trying to seek out information in a subject new to them, a particular type of literature, for example government publications, or a particular format, for example videotapes.

Each subject has its own structure and type of literature, and a guide can be used as a short cut to finding the information you are seeking. Particular forms of information source, for example pamphlets, videotapes and alternative journals, all have their own means of production, distribution and organization within libraries and information units. Knowledge of this will help the person seeking information.

When carrying out any information search it is worthwhile checking for an information guide on the particular topic as it can be used to identify useful information sources and it may also provide guidance on using particular sources.

There are some problems associated with literature guides:

1 they are out of date as soon as they are published;
2 they may be written for a particular audience, for example

librarians and information scientists, and assume a subject knowledge the user doesn't actually have;

3 they are likely to be biased, for example in terms of countries of origin of sources;

4 they may contain errors such as incomplete bibliographic citations or may miss important sources.

General literature guides

American Reference Books Annual (Littleton, Colorado: Libraries Unlimited, 1969–   ).
This book is divided into the following sections: general reference works; social sciences; humanities; and, finally, science and technology. The following sub headings are likely to contain items of interest to someone searching for information on the alternative therapies: education; library science, publishing and bookselling, psychology, sociology and health sciences.

Guide to Reference Material, 4th edn. Vol. 2, *Social and Historical Sciences, Philosophy and Religion.* Vol. 3, *Generalities, Languages, the Arts and Literature.* Edited by A. J. Walford (London: Library Association, 1982, 1986).
These two standard reference materials are a useful starting point in any literature search. For example, Volume 3 can be used to identify national bibliographies. These items have detailed indexes.

Guide to Reference Books, 10th edn. Edited by E. P. Sheehy (Chicago: American Library Association, 1987).
This book covers more than 14 000 reference works from around the world. Its coverage includes items published up to 1985. This is a standard reference tool.

Printed Reference Materials, 2nd edn. Edited by Gavin Higgens (London: Library Association, 1984).
This is a useful guide to reference materials and is divided into chapters which deal with different categories of material. Its emphasis is on mainstream resources.

Guides to particular forms of literature

Guides exist to particular forms of literature such as official publications, alternative publications, statistics and theses. As these types of literature can be quite difficult to track down, such guides can save the information searcher time. Guides to audiovisual and computerized resources are covered later in this chapter.

Guides to abstracting and indexing services

Inventory of Abstracting and Indexing Services Produced in the UK. By J.Stephens (London: British Library, 1986).

Guides to the alternative literature

Alternative Materials in Libraries. Edited by James P. Danky and Elliott Shore (Metuchen, NJ: Scarecrow, 1982).
This is a key guide to alternative materials and it is aimed at the librarian. It has an extensive bibliography which includes directories, bibliographies, indexes and handbooks. It includes older materials and retrospective finding tools which have not been included in the *Field Guide to Alternative Media* described below.

Field Guide to Alternative Media. A Directory to Reference and Selection Tools Useful in Accessing Small and Alternative Press Publications and Independently Produced Media. Edited and compiled by Patricia J. Case (Chicago: Task Force on Alternatives in Print, Social Responsibilities Round Table, American Library Association, 1984).
This small publication (it is an A4-sized pamphlet of 44 pages) contains a wealth of useful information. It is divided into the following sections: subject and trade directories; indices and subject bibliographies; trade and review media; bookstore and distributor catalogs; selective bibliography. There is a consolidated title, editor, media, publisher, bookseller and subject index.

Guides to bibliographies

An Annotated Guide to Current National Bibliographies. By Barbara L. Bell (Cambridge: Chadwyck-Healey, 1986).

Guide to Current National Bibliographies in the Third World. By G. E. Gorman and M. M. Mahoney (Oxford: Zell, 1983).

Guides to official publications

Bibliography of Official Statistical Yearbooks and Bulletins. By Gloria Westfall (Cambridge: Chadwyck-Healey, 1986).
Directory of British Official Publications, 2nd edn. Compiled by Stephen Richard (London: Mansell, 1984).
This book provides a guide to British official publications and has an organizations and subject index.

Guides to theses and dissertations

Guide to Theses and Dissertations: An International Annotated Bibliography of Bibliographies. By Michel M. Reynolds (Arizona: Oryx Press, 1986).

Guides to specialist subjects

I have not found any literature guides to the alternative therapies. The following guides contain information relevant to the field of alternative therapy:

How to Find Out in Psychiatry: A Guide to Sources of Mental Health Information. By B. Greenberg (Oxford: Pergamon, 1978).
How to Search for Information: A Beginner's Guide to the Literature of Psychology. By L. Greenwood (Lexington: Willowood, 1980).
Humanistic Psychology, a Guide to Information Sources. By Gloria Behar Gottsegen and Abby J. Gottsegen (Detroit: Gale, c1980).
Library Use: A Handbook for Psychology. By J. G. Reed and P. M. Baxter (Washington, DC: American Psychological Association, 1983).
Psychology of Religion: A Guide to Information Sources (Detroit, Michigan: Gale, 1976).
This book contains about 4000 annotated entries and is restricted to material published between 1950 and 1974. It is divided into sections which include: psychology of religion; ritual; social and directional dimensions of religion.

Research Guide for Psychology. By R. G. McInnis (London: Greenwood, 1982).

Women in America: A Guide to Information Sources. Edited by V. R. Terris (Detroit, Mich: Gale, 1980).
This is a useful source as it has a chapter on 'Health, mental health and sexuality' and covers alternative medicine and therapies. There are ten appendices which cover: centres; collections; film and audiovisual sources; government agencies; news and information services; newsletters; organizations; periodicals; presses; and reprint houses. There are author, title and subject indexes.

Women's Studies: A Checklist of Bibliographies. Compiled by M. Ritchie (London: Mansell, 1980).
This useful bibliography does contain some references of relevance to alternative therapy under the section headings: health and medicine; and psychology and psychiatry.

Dictionaries

The function of a dictionary is to help define and standardize the vocabulary in a given subject field or language. They are particularly useful when trying to search for information in a new field.
Relevant dictionaries include:

Dictionary of Behavioural Science. By B. B. Wolman (New York: Van Nostrand Reinhold, 1973).
This dictionary has about 10 000 entries which include brief biographies. The slant is American.

A Dictionary of Gestures. By Betty J. Bauml and Franz H. Bauml (Metuchen, NJ: Scarecrow, 1975).
This interesting book covers a vast array of gestures and provides geographic identification. There is a bibliography.

Dictionary of Key Words in Psychology. By Frank J. Bruno (London: Routledge & Kegan Paul, 1986).
This is an extremely useful dictionary which contains clear definitions and illustrations. It also contains entries on individual psychologists and therapists.

62

The Therapist's Thesaurus: A Cartoon Guide. By Robert Wilkins and Penny Loudon (London: Croom Helm, c1987).
This is an interesting and informative book.

Encyclopedias

Encyclopedias are publications which attempt to cover established subject knowledge either in a particular field, such as:

The Encyclopedia of Alternative Medicine and Self-Help. Edited by Malcolm Hulke (London: Rider, 1978).

or the whole of knowledge, such as:

Encyclopedia Britannica (Chicago: Encyclopedia Britannica, 1975).

The aim of encyclopedias is to provide the reader with a summary of a particular topic. General encyclopedias, for example *Encyclopedia Britannica*, have a limited use for anyone searching the field of alternative therapy
Specialist encyclopedias can be used to provide concise information on a particular subject, for example alternative therapy.

The Encyclopedia of Alternative Medicine and Self-Help, listed above, provides a wealth of information on both alternative medicine and therapies.
This publication is divided into two parts: encyclopedia and directory. The encyclopedia proper provides detailed descriptions of different types of therapy and each description is written by an expert in the field. Cross-references indicated by bold typescript refer the user to other therapies. At the end of each entry are references to the appropriate sections of the second part – the directory – of the book, and in some cases a brief bibliography.
The directory contains the following details:

Associations and societies: name; address; telephone number; secretary/director/principal/founder; journal (name, frequency, contents); aims; reference to entry in encyclopedia.
Contributors: name; qualifications; address; telephone number. Arranged in alphabetical order under subject. Not all contributors are listed.

Products: name of organization; address; name of product; description; cost.

Training centres: name; address; principal; courses.

Health farms: name; address; telephone number; director; capacity; fees; treatment; location; facilities.

Health magazines: name; frequency; publisher; address; telephone number. This section does not cover those publications listed under Associations and societies.

Festival: details of the Festival for Mind and Body held annually in London.

Speakers: directs the user to the sections on Contributors and Associations and societies and also a publication Speakers International.

Bibliography: a short reading list is arranged under subject headings. The majority of references refer to books.

This book provides a useful guide to alternative therapies but it is now out of date and so directory entries should to be treated with caution.

International Encyclopedia of Psychiatry, Psychology, Psychoanalysis & Neurology. Edited by B. B. Wolman (New York: Van Nostrand Reinhold, 1977). Twelve volumes.
This is an immense work which, despite taking a traditional approach to the field, contains much useful information, particularly historical, on alternative therapies.

The Practical Encyclopedia of Natural Healing. By Mark Bricklin (Emmaus, PA: Rodale Press, 1983).
This is a useful resource containing many full-length articles which are well indexed. The book is written in a readable style.

A Visual Encyclopedia of Unconventional Medicine. Edited by Ann Hill (London: New English Library, 1979).
As its name suggests, this encyclopedia is fully illustrated. It is divided into the following sections: comprehensive systems (for example oriental medicine); diagnostic methods; physical therapies – meridian therapies, manipulative and muscle retraining, heat, air and light, electrotherapy, mineral contact; hydrotherapy; plant-based therapies; nutrition; wave, radiation and vibration; mind and spirit therapies; self-exercise therapies. Each section is written by

an 'expert' and the book contains a detailed bibliography and resource list. The book provides a useful guide to alternative therapies but it is now out of date and so some of the information it contains should be treated with caution.

Directories

A directory is a reference tool that can be used to find information on people or organizations. Directories are signposts to other sources of information and can be used to make short cuts in a search for information. One of the best-known directories is the telephone directory.

Guides to directories

Guides to directories exist and these can be used to track down a relevant directory.

Directory of Directories, 2nd edn. By James Etheridge (Detroit: Gale Research, 1983).
This directory contains details of other directories and its bias is towards American publications. This directory is divided into three sections: the directory; a title index; a subject index. Information contained in each entry includes: title, publisher (with address and telephone number), coverage, description of the entries, arrangement, indexes, number of pages, frequency and prices.

International Bibliography of Special Directories, 7th edn. Edited by Helga Lengenfelder (Munich: K. G. Saur, 1983).
This item lists more than 6000 directories which are published irregularly or regularly in about fifty countries worldwide. It is divided into the following sections: general directories; cultural affairs, arts, sciences and technology; state and society; commerce and industry; individuals; classified list of trade and industries; public transportation and transport; communications. As it lacks a subject or title index it is difficult to use and it would be easy to miss relevant items. If you are searching for a directory it is worth including this one as a search tool as it does contain details of directories which are otherwise difficult to find such as:

International Psychic Register. Edited by Donal A. McQuaid (Erie:

Orion Press, 1980-). An annual publication with approximately 1000 entries.

Top 2000 Directories and Annuals 1984/1985, 5th edn. Edited by Jane Eden (Reading: Alan Armstrong, 1984). Previously called *Top 1000 Directories and Annuals.*

This directory is divided into five sections which are printed on different coloured paper for easy usage.

Part 1   Alphabetical listing of directories and annuals. Title order. White pages.

Part 2   New publications first issued since January 1983. Blue pages.

Part 3   List of directories and annuals by month of issue. Blue pages.

Part 4   List of publishers and their directories and annuals. Yellow pages.

Part 5   Subject index. Pink pages.

Each entry contains the following information: title; current edition; next edition; ISBN; editor; subject coverage. This directory provides a useful guide to a whole variety of directories, some of which are relevant to alternative therapy: *Alternatives in Print* and *Associations' Publications in Print* (see 'General sources').

The Whole Again Resource Guide, 1986/87. By Tim Ryan, Patricia J. Case and others (Santa Barbara, CA: SourceNet, 1986).

This is one of the most important guides to alternative and new age periodicals and resource books. It covers: journals and newspapers; abstracting and indexing services; handbooks; bibliographies; and other source books. While there is a chapter on directories, many directories are listed in the subject sections such as astrology, body-work, holistic health, mindwork, new age, psychic studies. The coverage of this book is biased towards English language materials but it also includes materials in other languages.

The chapters are arranged in alphabetical order from 'Alternative news' to 'Yoga', and this is followed by sections called 'Where else to look, 'Finding a practitioner', and an 'Epilog'. Each section is clearly labelled and begins with an illustration and brief introduction to the subject, followed by the directory entries arranged alphabetically. Each entry contains the following information:

Entry number
Title
Publisher
Address   Editor
                                 Phone
Frequency   Size
Highlights   ISSN/ISBN
Description

The end of each chapter contains a list of resource books including directories and catalogues relevant to that subject.

The directory has a geographic index (which is arranged by state within the USA, by province within Canada, and then alphabetically by country), and an index which lists editors and authors, issuing organizations and publishers, titles and subjects.

This is one of the most useful directories that I have come across with respect to finding information sources on the alternative therapies. It is visually interesting to look at and very easy to use.

Useful directories

It would be impossible to describe every directory which is relevant to people looking for information on alternative therapy. In this section, I have selected some key directories.

General directories Under this heading, I have listed directories which are most commonly found in libraries and which may be of some help to people searching for information on the alternative therapies.

ASLIB Directory of Information Sources in the United Kingdom, 5th edn. Edited by Ellen M. Codlin (London: ASLIB, 1984).
This is a useful general guide to anyone searching for specialized information sources, for example special libraries. Volume 2 covers the social sciences, medicine and the humanities. It is an alphabetical listing of more than 3600 organizations. See also *The Shorter ASLIB Directory of Information Sources in the United Kingdom.*

Directory of British Associations, 7th edn. (Beckenham, Kent: CBD Research, 1982).
This directory is an important source of information about associ-

ations, societies, charities and self-help groups. The arrangement within the directory is alphabetical by subject with a subject index. The entry in the subject index under 'therapy' directs the reader to 'individual forms of therapy'. There is a useful abbreviations index and this can be used to identify organizations. For example, on checking this index for BHA the following entries are found:

British Hardmetal Association
British Homeopathic Association
British Humanist Association
British Hypnotherapy Association

The required entry can then be found in the alphabetical section of the directory.

Directory of European Associations (Part 1: *National Trade and Professional Associations,* 1981; Part 2: *National Learned, Scientific and Technical Associations,* 2nd edn, 1979) (Beckenham, Kent: CBD Research).
This is a companion directory to the *Directory of British Associations*. There are subject, organization and abbreviations indexes. The entries are arranged by subject and within each subject by country.

DITTO. Directory of Independent Training and Tutorial Organizations. By Elizabeth Summerson and Maureen Davies (Richmond: Career Consultants Ltd, 1985).
While the *World of Learning* covers conventional organizations, *DITTO* provides access to independent 'alternative' bodies which offer education and training on particular subjects. This directory begins with an introductory section which covers: place of independent training and tutorial organizations in further education; checklist for choosing a course; finance; notes for overseas students; correspondence and home study courses; self-employment; and sources of further information. The rest of the book is divided into sections according to subject and 'therapy' falls under the heading 'health and beauty'.

The heading 'health and beauty' is divided into sections: Section 1 covers 'counselling, psychotherapy, hypnosis and other related therapies'; Section 2 covers personality analysis and contains entries under astrology, and graphology; Section 3 covers alternative medicine and includes entries for massage, postural integration and pulsing.

Each section contains two types of entry: full entries which include name, address, courses offered and any special notes; and brief entries, that is, names and addresses of organizations and individuals believed to be offering training courses currently, but from whom it was not possible to obtain full information.

This directory contains two indexes: training and tutorial organizations, and a subject index. The latter includes broad subject headings, for example artistic therapy, massage, meditation and psychotherapy, but does not cover all the subjects covered in the directory, for example postural integration is missing.

The actual number of entries relating to alternative therapy is low, which reduces the value of this tool for someone looking for information on courses in this field. See Chapter 9 for alternative sources of this information.

Encyclopedia of Associations, 14th edn. Edited by Nancy Yakes and Denise Akey (Detroit, Michigan: Gale Research, 1980).
This is published in four volumes: Volume 1 covers US organizations; Volume 2 is a geographic and executive index; Volume 3 is a periodical supplement of new associations and societies; and Volume 4 is a bibliography, name index and subject index. Volume 1 is most commonly found in libraries in the UK. This is a very useful source of information and below is an example entry:

9412
INSTITUTE FOR RATIONAL LIVING (Psychotherapy)(IRL)
45 E 65th St.   Phone: (212) 535–0822
New York, NY 10021   Albert Ellis, Ph.D., Exec.Dir.
Founded: 1959. Members: 2000. Staff: 15. Regional groups: 6.
Psychologists, psychiatrists, social workers, counselors, other professionals and laypeople practising or interested in rational-emotive psychotherapy. Believes that emotional disturbance is due primarily to currently held irrational attitudes and beliefs about the nature of one's self and the social environment. Provides lectures and workshops for the general public; a speakers bureau; publications division; referral service to psychotherapists in the US and Canada. Maintains library of 3000

volumes. Publications: (1) Rational living, semiannual; (2) News-letter, annual; (3) Publications list, annual; also distributes books, pamphlets and tape recordings. Affiliated with: Institute for Rational Emotive Therapy. Convention/Meeting: annual – 1980 New York City.

The Shorter ASLIB Directory of Information Sources in the United Kingdom. Edited by Ellen M. Codlin (London: ASLIB, 1986).
This book provides a listing of libraries and information units in central government, local authorities, universities and polytechnics, learned, professional and research institutions, commercial and industrial bodies, as well as frequently needed specialized sources. There is a detailed subject index which can be used to find items relevant to alternative therapies, for example there are two entries under psychotherapy. A typical entry contains the following details:

364 CENTRE FOR THE STUDY OF ALTERNATIVE THERAPIES

51 Bedford Place, Southampton SO1 2DG Tel: 0703 334752
Training and research body.
Enquiries direct to the Centre.
Subject coverage
acupuncture; osteopathy; clinical ecology (food and chemical sensitivity); homeopathy; Alexander technique; psycho-therapy; relaxation techniques; hypnosis.

Trade Associations and Professional Bodies of the United Kingdom, 8th edn. Edited by Patricia Millard (Oxford: Pergamon, 1987).
World of Learning 1983–1984, 34th edn (London: Europa, 1983).
This directory is a very useful source of information about educational activities around the world. For each country there are entries under the following headings – academies, learned societies, research institutes, libraries and archives, museums and art galleries, and universities and colleges. There is also a section on international bodies such as the World Health Organization. This book is easy to use if one is searching by country or by institution. Subject searching is more time-consuming as there is no separate subject index.

Specialist directories   The directories listed here cover either alternative materials and activities, or counselling and therapy agencies and organizations. They are less likely to be found in libraries than the directories listed above but they are more likely to provide information on the alternative therapies.

Alternative America. Edited by Richard Gardner (Cambridge, MA: Alternative America, 1984).
This book covers 13 000 organizations and publishers. It is a poorly arranged directory as entries are arranged in zip code order with organization, title, and subject indexes. Its subject coverage does include the alternative therapies.

Alternative Visions (Kitchener, Ontario: Alternative Research). Biannual.
This is a typed directory to alternative resources which covers the following: organizations; books; directories; guides; bibliographies; indexes; alternative shops; and games.

The Directory of Complementary and Alternative Practitioners 1987–88. Compiled and edited by Michael C. Williams (Colyton, Devon: Health Farm Publishing, 1987-).
This is a key source for anyone searching for information on alternative therapies in the UK despite the emphasis being on alternative medicine and the omission of some psychological therapies. The next edition is planned for 1988. This directory lists over 4000 persons and healing centres involved in alternative health care in the UK and includes over 350 organizations, societies and colleges. There is also a diary of events – workshops, lectures, conferences.

The book begins with an introduction to alternative medicine and this is followed by detailed instructions on how to use the directory. Under the heading 'Beware of the quack' readers are given practical advice on finding an alternative practitioner. Next comes a list of designatory letters – invaluable to anyone wishing to check on the qualifications of a practitioner.

This is followed by a bulky section (66 pages) on the therapies, comprising an alphabetical listing of the following therapies:

Acupuncture; Alexander technique; allergy; aromatherapy; Bach flower remedies; body tuning and resonance therapy; cancer therapy; chiropractic; colour therapy; electro-crystal therapy; spiritual healing; herbal medicine; homeopathy; hypnotherapy; iridology; kinesiology; magnetic therapy; therapeutic massage; music therapy; naturopathy; nutrition; organic food; osteopathy; polarity therapy; psychotherapy; radionics; rebirthing; reflexology; reiki; rolfing; Shiatsu; spinal touch; yoga; miscellaneous; multi-therapy.

The main part of the book (384 pages) is a practitioner listing. This is arranged by county and within each section alphabetically by practitioner name with a place and therapy index, and an events listing. The final sections of the book include an events diary and postal services.

Handbuch zur Information und Kontaktaufnahme in der Alternativen Szene. Compiled by Das Addressbuch Alternativer Projekte (Klingelbach, W Germany: Mandala Verlag Peter Meyer). Annual. This directory lists organizations and publications from Germany and 223 other countries. The subject coverage includes alternative health, therapy and spiritual development. Entries provide names, addresses, telephone numbers and a brief description. The text is in German with English annotations for organizations and publications from English- speaking countries.

The Health Information Handbook. Resources for Self Care. By Robert Gann (Aldershot: Gower, 1986).
This handbook offers practical guidance to the library services, advice centres, voluntary and self-help groups, and health professionals on the provision of health information to the public. This useful book provides detailed guidance on the resources and services in the UK, with overviews of the current situation in many other countries. While primarily concerned with traditional health care information the book includes many resources which are likely to be of interest to people searching for information on alternative therapy.

Healthsharing Book: Resources for Canadian Women. Edited by Kathleen McDonnell and Mariana Valverde (Toronto: Women's Press, c1985).
This book covers women's health, including alternative health and therapy, and provides a useful resources listing.

The Institute of Complementary Medicine Yearbook (London: Foulsham, 1986–).
This is a useful source of information. The directory is divided into sections:

Professional associations under subject, for example acupuncture
Postal services
Organizations list – national list under subject
                              – regional list by county
Guide to qualifications
Careers in complementary medicine – training colleges

Information is clearly presented and the Institute of Complementary Medicine offers a back-up information service which will provide further information and also give details of changes in contacts for organizations.

New Age Directory: Holistic Health Guide. Edited by Victoria Kulvinskas (Fairfield, IA: Omangood Press, 1981).
This directory has over 3700 entries and these are comprehensively indexed by subject, keyword, and state. There is a rather complicated classification scheme but this directory can be used to track down growth centres, healing centres and others in the USA.

New Consciousness Sourcebook. By Parmatma Singh Khalsa (Berkeley, CA: Spiritual Community Publications, 1982).
This resource guide is divided into four parts: New consciousness centres; Articles and resources; Community directory – USA, Canada, Mexico and overseas; Classified listings – from astrology to yoga and meditation.

New Life Directory (Lydebrook, Forest of Dean: Soluna Publications, 1982–).
This publication provides an alphabetical guide to healing centres, publishers, communities, festivals and associations in the UK. Each entry includes name, address, telephone number, contact person and a detailed description of the group. There is a map showing the location of the directory entries.

A Pilgrim's Guide to Planet Earth. Edited by Parmatma Singh Khalsa (San Rafael, CA: Spiritual Community Publications, 1981).
This is a comprehensive resource guide to alternative bookshops,

73

growth centres, and spiritual centres around the world. The arrangement is geographic by country and there are no indexes.

Someone to Talk to Directory 1985. Compiled by Penny Webb (London; Mental Health Foundation; distributed by Routledge & Kegan Paul, 1985).
This is a vast directory which covers many subject areas – some of them of interest to people looking for information on alternative therapy. The directory is divided into sections and the section headings relate to either a 'problem' area, for example addiction, or services and agencies, for example 'complementary medicine', counselling services, education, women's organizations. The section called complementary medicine has a subheading 'alternative medicine and the natural therapies' which includes a long list of topics, including advice and information, astrology, research, retreats and yoga. Under each topic are entries for 'UK – National' and these are followed by 'UK – Local'. Below is an example of a typical entry:

London Institute of Postural Integration
C/o 18 Park Hill Road,
CROYDON
Surrey CR0 5NA
Tel: 01–680 4660
Open during office hours
3 6 9 13 15 17
Runs six-week courses in postural integration and pulsing. Contact the centre for details.

A key at the bottom of each page indicates the meaning of the numeric code, for instance 6 = SAE required, 13 = referral service. There is a detailed subject index. This is an extrememly valuable directory which covers many important sources.

Thorsons' Complete Guide to Alternative Living. By David Harvey (Wellingborough: Thorsons, 1986).
The first section of this directory is an A–Z listing of the ideas, beliefs and philosophies behind alternative therapies, education, politics and other aspects of the alternative movement. The entries are informative and include references. The second section is a

74

directory of organizations in the UK and overseas. Entries are divided under the following subject headings: health; self-development centres; new age organizations; astrology, psychic research and other groups.

Specialized alternative therapy directories The directories described above all cover one or more subjects included in alternative therapy. Many specialist bodies and societies also produce directories, for example of practitioners in their field. These include:

AHP Resource Guide (San Francisco: Association for Humanistic Psychology, 1984).
This is a directory of members, their skills and special interest areas. There are alphabetical and geographic indexes.

A Referral Directory of Individual Counsellors, 3rd edn. Edited by Donald Godden (Rugby: British Association of Counselling, 1983). In this directory entries are arranged under geographical headings, by counties of the UK. Each entry contains the following information: name and address of counsellor; relevant professional training and qualifications; whether the counsellor works with individuals, couples, families or groups; any special problems dealt with; the kind(s) of therapy used; any supervision they have; and whether medical support is available; time(s) they are available; fees; membership of any division of the BAC. This is a very concise directory and much of the detail in it is abbreviated though there is a useful key to abbreviations, for example:

GF   guided fantasy
th   therapy
spir   spiritual.

There is also an index to names. This is a useful source which is updated at regular intervals.

Directories are also available which provide a guide to one or more kinds of therapy over a particular geographic location, e.g.

Leeds Healing Network Internal Register (Leeds: Leeds Healing Network, 1987–   ).

This register contains details of therapists and healers working in the Leeds area. It is an internal publication but the group has plans to use it as the basis of an external register. The register is divided into sections according to subject. Each section starts with a description of the method of therapy or healing, followed by a list of practitioners. For each practitioner the following details are included: name; address; telephone number; membership of professional bodies and training; charges.

Local Directory for Complementary Medicine. Volume 1: *Practitioners,*. Volume 2: *Background Information* (Huddersfield; Wholistic Health and Life Enterprises, c1987).
This directory provides information about therapists in Huddersfield and surrounding towns in the North of England and it is presented in A4 format in two volumes. The first contains a brief introduction; a clear guide to using the directory; the directory – a list of practitioners arranged under type of therapy; information – local networks, national organizations; and a glossary.

The second volume contains information about therapy and contains copies of journal articles, book lists and advertising material. It is a fascinating collection of material which gives a good overview of the world of therapy.

Who's Who in the Healing Arts. Edited by Julia von Erffa Gregg (Santa Fe, NM: The Referral Service for Health Care Information, 1985).
This directory is arranged by subject and lists practitioners in Santa Fe and other parts of New Mexico. Each field of work is described and the practitioner entries include details of what each is offering.

Bibliographies

A bibliography is a list of printed or non-printed materials (such as videotapes, films, games, or computer programs) which has been produced by an individual, a group or an organization. Bibliographies can be an important source of information but a problem with those in this field is that their coverage may be restricted to mainstream works and avoid the alternative literature.

There are a number of different types of bibliographies which are of relevance to people searching for information on the alternative therapies: general bibliographies; general therapy bibliographies; and specialized bibliographies.

General bibliographies

General bibliographies are those which may cover the whole field of knowledge or represent the publications of a particular country or in a particular language. Examples include national bibliographies such as that produced by the British Library (*British National Bibliography*) and bibliographies produced by a commercial organization such as *Books in Print* from Bowker in New York and library catalogues. These bibliographies can be tracked down using standard reference works such as Sheehy's *Guide to Reference Works* and Walford's *Guide to Reference Material.* Examples include:

American Book Publishing Record (New York: Bowker, 1960–).
Books in Print (New York: Bowker, 1948–).
British Books in Print (London: Whitaker, 1974–).
British National Bibliography (London: British Library, 1950–).
International Books in Print (New York: Saur, 1985).

General bibliographies of alternative materials are likely to be helpful and examples include:

Information America: A Guide to Print and Nonprint Materials Available from Organizations, Government Agencies, and Specialized Publishers. Edited by Tracy Davis (New York: Neal Schuman). Three per year.
This directory covers materials published by organizations whose main objective is not publishing, and also from highly specialized publishers. It includes materials which may otherwise be hard to track down. There are title and subject indexes.

Small Press Record of Books in Print. Edited by Len Fulton (Paradise, CA: Dustbooks). Annual.
This is the US alternative books in print. Entries are arranged under subject headings with a brief bibliographic description and annotation. There are subject, title and publisher indexes. This is a very useful reference tool.

Sources: A Guide to Print and Nonprint Materials Available from

Organizations, Industry, Government Agencies and Specialized Publishers (Syracuse, NY: Gaylord, 1977–). Three per year.
Lists about 2000 US and Canadian publications which come from organizations which publish but are not publishers *per se.* Title and annual subject index.

Vertical File Index: A Subject and Title Index to Selected Pamphlet Material (New York: Wilson, 1932–). Monthly.
Previously called *Vertical File Service Catalog.* Arranged by subject with a title index.

Whole Again Resource Guide, 1986/87. Edited by Tim Ryan, Patricia J. Case and others (Santa Barbara, CA: SourceNet, 1986). This is a key guide for anyone searching for information on the alternative therapies. This book covers: periodicals and newsletters; directories; audiovisual materials; abstracting services; and bibliographies. It is divided into chapters and the following are relevant to this field: alternative news; astrology; bodywork; channelling; communications; death; directories; exercise; holistic health; mindwork; psychic studies; spiritual growth; yoga; where else to look; and finding a practitioner. There is a geographic index and a combined author, editor, organization, publisher, subject and title index. The book is very well presented and contains a wealth of information. Its coverage is international though biased towards English-speaking countries and publications.

Some subject bibliographies are likely to have a wide coverage of therapy books. Examples include:

Alternative Medicine. Compiled by Ruth West and Joanna E. Trevelyan (London: Mansell, 1985).
This book is chiefly concerned with homeopathy, herbal medicine, naturopathy, clinical nutrition, osteopathy, chiropractic, Chinese medicine, and acupuncture. However, it contains entries, particularly in the introduction, of interest to alternative therapists. Its coverage is restricted to books and includes items from both the nineteenth and twentieth centuries.

Bibliographic Guide to Psychology (Boston, Mass: Research Libraries of the New York Public Library and the Library of Congress, 1974–).

This bibliography is published annually and lists all materials cata-logued during the previous year by the NYPL Research Libraries as well as items from the Library of Congress MARC tapes. The coverage is not restricted to 'traditional' psychology but includes alternative approaches, parapsychology and the occult sciences. The 1974 volume covers the Library of Congress accessions only.

General therapy bibliographies

Books for Inner Development. The YES! Bookshop Guide. By Cris Popenoe (Washington, DC: YES! Bookshop, 1976).
This was one of the first published bibliographies in the field of inner growth and therapy. It was superseded by the revised edition, *Inner Development. . . .* – which is described below.

Inner Development. The YES! Bookshop Guide. By Cris Popenoe (Harmondsworth: Penguin, 1979).
This book is an expanded and revised edition of *Books for Inner Development* and is an important and comprehensive guide to the literature in this field. It covers a vast range of topics – from African philosopies via dreams and humanistic psychology to women and men. Excluded topics – holistic health, nutrition, and bodywork – can be found in the companion volume *Wellness. The YES! Bookshop Guide.* The book is arranged in subject order, with an author index, and there is a very useful guide to publishers, which includes details of publishers who are difficult to track down.

Mind–Body Therapies. A Select Bibliography of Books in English. By Robin Monro, Joanna E. Trevelyan and Ruth West (London: Mansell, 1987).
This bibliography covers over 1180 books in English and entries are arranged under the following subject headings: yoga; hypno-therapy; Alexander technique; autogenic training; biofeedback; acupressure and Shiatsu; applied kinesiology; reflexology/zone therapy/metamorphic technique; aromatherapy; Bach flower remedies; and tissue salts. There are author, title and subject indexes.

Self-Help: 1400 Best Books on Personal Growth. By Bill Katz and Linda Katz Sternberg (NY; London: Bowker, 1985).

A Therapist's Bibliography. By Derek Gale (Loughton, Essex: Gale Centre Publications, 1987).
This publication is divided into three parts: 'Books which changed my life' – an autobiographical account of books which have been important to the author's personal development; 'Some of the books on my shelf'; and finally a list of books, journals and addresses. The second section is divided into the following parts: books on individual psychotherapy; books on groups, group psychotherapy and group work; guides to therapy; daisies (books on selected topics). The main problem with this book is found in the third section (the bibliography proper) as the author has not included publisher details or date of publication and this means that some of the items in it are likely to be difficult to trace. This is a pity as the bibliography provides a useful introductory guide to the world of therapy.

Wellness. The YES! Bookshop Guide. By Cris Popenoe (Washington, DC: YES! Bookshop, 1977).
This is a bibliography of more than 1500 entries which are arranged under the following headings: anatomy and physiology; body work; colour and aura; cookbooks; healing; herbs; homeopathy; life energies; natural childbirth; nutrition; organic gardening, and oriental medicine.

Specialized bibliographies

Specialized bibliographies cover a small field of knowledge and examples include:

Alchemy: A Bibliography of English-Language Writings. By Alan Pritchard (London: Routledge & Kegan Paul, 1980).
This bibliography is arranged by country and subject. Topics covered of interest to alternative therapists include astrology, tarot and psychology (chiefly Jungian).

Astrology: A Comprehensive Bibliography. Edited by Cris Popenoe (Washington, DC: YES! Bookshop, 1982).
This bookshop catalogue lists about 1000 books on astrology in subject order. Full bibliographic details and an annotation are included for each entry. There is no index.

Astrology, Mysticism and the Occult. By Laird Wilcox (Kansas City: Editorial Research Service, 1980).
This is a critical bibliography of over 400 books and articles which are intended to expose fallacies in these subjects.

Body Movement and Nonverbal Communication: An Annotated Bibliography, 1971–1981. By Martha Davis and Janet Skupien (Bloomington, IN: Indiana University Press, 1982).
This book covers more than 1400 published works on psychological and anthropological aspects of body movement. There are author and subject indexes. See also *Understanding Body Movement, an Annotated Bibliography.*

International Meditation Bibliography, 1950–1982. By Howard R. Jarrell (Metuchen, NJ: Scarecrow, 1985).
This is a partly annotated bibliography which covers the following subjects: Christian meditation; Zen Buddhist meditation; relaxation techniques; yoga meditation; and transcendental meditation. It covers the following types of sources: periodicals; books; dissertations and theses; films; sound recordings; societies and associations. It has an author, title and subject index.

International Yoga Bibliography. By Howard Jarrell (Metuchen, NJ: Scarecrow, 1981).
This is a bibliography of 1731 entries – books, journals and magazine articles. The listings are arranged by author, title and subject. The entries are not annotated.

Jungian Psychology: A Comprehensive Guide. Edited by Cris Popenoe (Washington, DC: YES! Bookshop, 1982).
This bibliography covers over 250 books which are either by or about Carl Jung. Full bibliographic details are provided.

Mind and Immunity: Behavorial Immunology. By Stephen Locke (New York: Institute for the Advancement of Health, 1983).
This is an annotated bibliography with over 1300 entries.

Occult Bibliography: An Annotated List of Books Published in English, 1971 through 1975. By Thomas C. Clarie (Metuchen, NJ: Scarecrow, 1978). Also *Occult/Paranormal Bibliography: An Annotated List of Books Published in English, 1976 through 1981.* By Thomas C. Clarie (Metuchen, NJ: Scarecrow, 1984).

These two items provide a comprehensive bibliography of English language materials and contain many entries of interest to alternative therapists such as astrology and tarot.

Parapsychology: Sources of Information. By Rhea A. White and Laura A. Dale (Metuchen, NJ: Scarecrow, 1973).

Reading Therapy. Edited by Jean M. Clarke and Eileen Bostle (London: Bingley, to be published 1988).

Research in Ritual Studies. By Ronald L. Grimes (Metuchen, NJ: Scarecrow, 1985).
This book is divided into two sections: an essay which presents a state-of-the-art report on this interdisciplinary subject and evaluates some of the items in the bibliography; a bibliography which is grouped under four main headings – ritual components, ritual types, ritual descriptions, and general works.

Unconscious: A Guide to Sources. By Natalino Caputi (Metuchen, NJ: Scarecrow, 1985).
This book presents a bibliography which divides materials into four categories: the bio-physical approach; the psycho-personal approach; the socio-cultural approach; and the transpersonal-spiritual approach.

Understanding Body Movement, an Annotated Bibliography. By Davis Martha (New York: Arno, 1972).
This book contains almost 1000 abstracts and concentrates on English language titles. It includes dissertations and there is a subject index. See also *Body Movement and Nonverbal Communication. . .*

Abstracting and indexing services

Each year thousands of articles on alternative therapy are published in hundreds of journals. It would be an almost impossible task for anyone to read all these journals. Abstracting and indexing journals exist to provide signposts to the journal literature. One difficulty with searching for information on the alternative therapies is that periodical articles on it may be scattered through a range of disciplines and types of literature. In this section, eight different groups of abstracting and indexing services are looked at:

Alternative literature services
Educational services
Medical services
Psychology services
Religious and spiritual services
Social science services
Women's studies services
Current awareness services.

Alternative literature services

Alternative Press Index: An Index to Alternative and Radical Publications (Baltimore: Alternative Press Centre, 1969–).
API is a quarterly index and is one of the most important indexes of alternative press magazines and newspapers. It is a subject index and the indexing terms are taken from the source documents. Its subject coverage includes the alternative therapies.

The New Periodicals Index. Edited by Michael Haldeman (Boulder, CA: The Mediaworks, 1977–).
This index has been published annually since 1979 and it covers many new age publications (some of them not indexed elsewhere). There are author and subject indexes.

Parapsychology Abstracts International. Edited by Rhea White (Dix Hills, NY: Parapsychology Sources of Information Center, 1983–).
This abstracting journal is published twice a year and covers the following materials: journals; conference proceedings; chapters in books; books; dissertations and theses. It is international in its coverage and has author, title and subject indexes.

Educational services

British Education Index (London: British Library, 1954–).
This quarterly publication indexes approximately 140 British journals.

Current Index to Journals in Education (New York: Macmillan, 1969–).

CIJE is produced monthly and indexes over 700 journals, including British ones. It is produced by ERIC (Educational Resources Information Centre) and as the subject index is based on the use of ERIC descriptors you will need a copy of the *Thesaurus of ERIC Descriptors* to help you find the relevant search terms (see Chapter 4).

Education Index (New York: H. W. Wilson, 1929–).
This is a monthly publication which has a bias towards the US literature.

Resources in Education. ERIC (Washington, DC: ERIC, 1975–).
This monthly publication was previously called *Research in Education*.

Medical services

Current Literature on Health Services (London: DHSS, 1973–). Monthly.
Previous title *Current Literature on Personal Social Services*. This is a useful resource for accessing materials generated within the NHS.

Excerpta Medica (Amsterdam: Excerpta Medica, 1946–).
This is an important abstracting service in the medical sciences and it is included here because it does cover the alternative therapies (when relevant articles are published in more traditional circles). It is published as forty-four separate abstract journals with two drug-related indexes. Excerpta Medica also publishes a *List of Journals Abstracted*, a *Guide to the Classification and Indexing Scheme* and an on-line thesaurus *MALIMET*.

A useful guide to using the printed source is *How to Use Index Medicus and Excerpta Medica.* By Barry Strickland-Hodge (Aldershot: Gower, 1986).

Health Service Abstracts (London: DHSS). Monthly.
This monthly bulletin is available from the DHSS and is produced from the DHSS-DATA database. Each issue contains entries under broad subject headings. There are subject and author indexes.

Health Visitors Association Current Awareness Bulletin (London: Health Visitors Association). Quarterly.

Despite its title, this publication appears quarterly and is useful for retrospective searching. It is a subject listing with brief abstracts.

Index Medicus (Bethseda: National Library of Medicine, 1879–). This is one of the most important indexing services in the medical sciences and, like *Excerpta Medica*, it is included here because it does cover the alternative therapies. It is published monthly with an annual cumulation. There are comprehensive indexes and guides to the terminology used within *Index Medicus* such as *Medical Subject Headings* or *Public MeSH*. The on-line version of this source is called *Medline* (see Chapter 4).
A useful guide to using the printed source is *How to Use Index Medicus and Excerpta Medica*. By Barry Strickland-Hodge (Aldershot: Gower, 1986.)

International Nursing Index Including Nursing Citation Index (New York: American Nurses Association, 1966–). Quarterly.
This item was previously called *Nursing Research Index*. It is easy to use as its organization is based on that of *MeSH*.

Popular Medical Index (Letchworth, Herts: Mede). Quarterly.
This is a valuable tool which covers periodical articles and books on health topics, positive health and alternative medicine. Its coverage includes not only the main medical and nursing journals but also a number of women's magazines.

Psychology services

Bulletin Signalétique. 390. Psychologie et Psychopathologie. Psychiatrie (Paris: Centre National de la Recherche Scientifique, 1961–). This abstracting service was formerly published quarterly and called *Bulletin Signalétique. 20. Psychologie. Pédagogie*. It is now published at monthly intervals and each issue has subject and author indexes. There are also annual cumulated indexes.

Psychological Abstracts (Washington, DC: American Psychological Association, 1927–).
This is published at monthly intervals with annual cumulations. It uses a fixed term indexing policy and publishes a *Thesaurus of Psychological Index Terms*. See Chapter 4.

A useful guide to this publication is *How to Use Psychological Abstracts and Biological Abstracts*. By Barbara Allan and Barry Strickland-Hodge (Aldershot: Gower, 1987).

Psychological Index: An Annual Bibliography of the Literature of Psychology and Cognate Subjects, 1894–1935, Vols. 1-42 (Princetown, NJ: Psychological Review, 1895–1936).
This is a classified subject index to 150 844 books and journal articles published during the period. There are author indexes but no subject index. It is succeeded by *Psychological Abstracts.*

Religious and spiritual services

Theological and Religious Index. Edited by G. P. Cornish (Harrogate, N Yorkshire: Theological Abstracting and Bibliographical Services (TABS), 1972–1978).
A mimeographed publication with about 1000 index entries each year. It is divided into subject sections which include sociology, medicine and psychology.

Social science services

Abstracts for Social Workers (New York: National Association of Social Workers, 1965–). Quarterly.
It covers about 200 journals. Items are arranged in classified order and there are subject and author indexes.

Applied Social Sciences Indexes and Abstracts (London: Library Association, 1987–).
ASSIA is a bi-monthly journal which covers the contents of over 500 English language periodicals. There is an annual cumulative volume.

Social Science Citation Index (Philadelphia: ISI, 1974–).
A useful tool which enables the reader to track down items which authors have cited. Its coverage is very broad. This item is computer-produced and can be quite difficult to use.

Social Service Abstracts (London: HMSO, 1972–). Monthly.
This publication has a bias towards materials originating from the

UK and it covers DHSS circulars. It has annual cumulated subject indexes.

Voluntary Forum Abstracts (London: National Council for Voluntary Organizations, 1982–). Bi-monthly.
This periodical covers the voluntary sector in detail. It occasionally has entries of relevance to alternative therapy. It includes detailed abstracts, with subject, author, title and organization indexes.

Women's studies services

Women's Studies Abstracts (New York: Rush, 1972–). Quarterly.
Each entry contains about 200 abstracts on subjects which include: mental and physical health. This is a useful source for identifying items on 'women's therapy'.

Current awareness services

It may take three to six months (or longer) for a journal article to appear in an abstracting or indexing journal. Many people who are searching for articles want to get hold of up-to-date references. Current awareness journals fill the gap between the the publication of the original article and its inclusion in an abstracting and indexing journal. The journals frequently provide photocopies of the contents pages of journals with simple indexes. They are not intended for retrospective searching. Examples include:

BIMH Current Awareness Service (Kidderminster, Worcs: BIMH, 197?). Monthly.
This current awareness service covers book, journal articles, audiovisual materials and conferences in the field of mental handicap. It sometimes contains materials on alternative therapies.

British Library Lending Division Journal Contents Page Service (BLDSC, Boston Spa, W Yorkshire).
This service provides a photocopying service for journal contents pages. It is not a free service.

Community Currents (London: Community Projects Foundation). Bi-monthly.
Though this periodical is primarily concerned with community life

and action it includes health and related topics. It scans over 100 journals and also includes a selection of books and meetings. The subject coverage is similar to that of *Voluntary Forum Abstracts*.

Current Contents/Social and Behavioral Sciences (Philadelphia: ISI). Weekly.
This booklet contains facsimile copies of the current contents pages of selected journals in a particular field. The indexes include a list of journal issues covered, a weekly subject index, and an author and address index.

Health Education Council Resource Centre and Library Lists (London: Health Education Council). Free.
These free lists cover recent additions to the library, the resource centre and journal articles of interest to health educators. Alternative therapy is covered.

The Psychological Reader's Guide: An Easy-to-Scan Bibliographic Monthly, Listing the Contents of More than 200 Journals in Psychology (Lausanne: Elsevier, 1973–). Monthly.
This is a current awareness service. There are no indexes.

Periodicals

Periodicals are also called magazines, journals or serials. These publications may be published at regular or irregular periods and, generally speaking, with no envisaged date of cessation. In the field of alternative therapy, there are a variety of periodicals which range from 'academic' to 'esoteric' in their content.

Typical contents may include descriptive and informative reports, reflective discussions, case reports, review articles, news, details and reports of workshops and conferences, reviews of books, news of a particular society or of people, advertisements of workshops.

Periodicals may by published by traditional publishers, by co-operative groups (for example *Cahoots*), by societies (an example is *Counselling*), or by individuals (such as *Out From the Core*). Their bias is likely to reflect that of the publisher as well as the individual authors.

Use of periodicals

Periodicals are a useful means of keeping up to date with ideas and practices in a particular field. They can be used to identify people active in a particular subject and also identify networks and groups of people.

They are particularly relevant to research workers and students in a field as they can provide detailed background, theoretical and research information.

Guides to the periodical literature

If you are searching for a particular periodical there are a number of guides which may be of use.

Alternative Access Directory. Edited by Jack Wieder (Kentfield, CA: Catalyst Press, 1984).
This directory lists periodicals indexed in the *Alternative Press News* and also the newspapers in the Association of Alternative Newsweeklies. It also provides details of other contacts such as self-publishing groups, video and film groups.

Alternatives in Print. Edited by Jackie Eubanks (New York: Neal Schuman, 1980).
This directory has 23 000 entries which include details of publishers and listings of books, periodicals, newsletters and non-print materials.

Benn's Press Directory (Tonbridge, Kent: Benn). Annual.
Benn's is divided into sections which cover:

Newspapers
Free distribution newspapers
Periodicals, free magazines, directories, broadcasting
Agencies and service media
Organizations
Master index.

The periodicals section contains a classified index, and items relevant to the alternative therapies are found under the headings:

Alternative press
Health and hygiene
Medicine
Mental health
Sociology and social sciences
Welfare and social services
Yoga.

Periodicals are arranged in title order under these headings and each entry contains the following information:

Title
Date commenced
Number of publications/year
Subjects
Audience
Publisher
Editor
Circulation figures.

While this directory covers the 'alternative' literature coverage is not comprehensive as there are some omissions, for example the journal *Cahoots*.

Directory of British Alternative Periodicals, 1965–1974. Edited by J. Noyce (Hassocks, Sussex: Harvester Press, 1979).
An earlier edition of this book was titled *Smoothie's Directory of Alternative Media Periodicals*. The present edition covers 1256 titles which are arranged in A–Z order. It contains a wealth of information including: bibliographic description; some library holdings; personal name, place name. organization and subject indexes.

The Guide to Health-Oriented Periodicals, 2nd edn. By Jeff Breakey (Ashland, OR: Sprouting Publications, 1983).
This guide covers more than 250 periodicals which are arranged under subject headings such as holistic health, social transformation, global unity, and spiritual health. It includes titles which have ceased publication and there is a title and publisher name index.

International Directory of Little Magazines and Small Presses, 18th

edn. Edited by Len Fulton and Ellen Ferber (Paradise, CA: Dustbooks, 1982).
This annual directory lists small and special interest publishers and provides a great deal of information on scope and editorial policies plus geographical and subject indexes.

Irregular Serials and Annuals, 9th edn (New York and London: Bowker). Every two years.
This publication lists more than 34 000 serials published throughout the world. Like *Ulrich* its bias is towards academic serials and it covers those which are published less than twice a year or are classed as irregular. It covers periodicals, proceedings, transactions, 'advances in' series, reports, yearbooks, handbooks, annual reviews and monograph series. The organization and indexes are very similar to those in *Ulrich*.

Magazines for Libraries. Edited by Bill Katz and others (Ann Arbor: Bowker, 1986).
This directory is a buying guide for librarians and the entries are value-rated. It has the same format as *Ulrich's International Periodicals Directory* but it is selective in its choice of entries and includes only those publications that its editors consider to be good examples of their type.

Oxbridge Directory of Newsletters. Edited by Patricia Hagood (New York: Oxbridge Communications, 1986).
This directory lists over 9000 newsletters and has a title index. It is published by the National Association of Newsletters.

Standard Periodical Directory. Edited by Patricia Hagood (New York: Oxbridge Communications, 1985).
This is a periodical directory of items published in the USA and Canada, and it includes 65 000 entries. Each entry provides detailed information which includes circulation, advertising and format information. Its coverage is biased towards traditional publications but some alternative ones are also included.

Ulrich Online
See 'Computerized information sources' later in this chapter.

Ulrich's International Periodicals Directory (New York and London: Bowker). Every two years.

This is published every two years and it alternates with another Bowker publication *Irregular Serials and Annuals*. It is available in most libraries and provides a listing of journals in print. It covers more than 65 000 periodicals but its coverage is biased towards academic periodicals. Many publications from the alternative press are missing.

As from 1983 it has been published in two volumes: Volume 1 is a classified listing covering subjects A–M, Volume 2 covers N–Z and also contains the following information: periodicals available on-line; vendor listing/periodicals on-line; cessations; index to publications of international organizations; title index.

The journals it does cover are arranged in subject order under one of over 500 subject headings. Items of interest to people searching for information on alternative therapy are likely to be found under the subject headings: psychology; medical sciences – psychiatry and neurology; social sciences. Cross-references are used to direct the reader to a particular entry when it could be classified under more than one topic.

Ulrich's Quarterly (New York and London: Bowker). Quarterly.
This provides up-to-date information on periodicals and serials which are published between the editions of *Ulrich's International Periodicals Directory* and *Irregular Serials and Annuals*. Its structure is similar to the two main directories.

The Underground and Alternative Press in Britain During 1973: A Bibliographic Guide: A Title and Chronological Index to the Underground-Alternative Press Microform Collection (Hassocks, Sussex: Harvester, 1975).

US Progressive Periodicals Directory (Nashville, TN: Progressive Education Service of the South, 1982).
A subject listing of 380 periodicals with basic subscription information and addresses.

Walford's Guide to Current British Periodicals in the Humanities and Social Sciences. Edited by A. J. Walford (London: Library Association, 1985).
This is a useful and easy to read guide to periodicals and magazines published in Britain. It is divided into sections according to the

UDC (Universal Decimal Classification) scheme. Entries relevant to alternative therapy can be found under the following sections:

0 Generalia
  04/05 Theses, reports, reviews. General periodicals
  06/09 Conferences . . .
1 Philosophy & Psychology
2 Religion
3 Social Sciences
7 The Arts

Each section begins with a list of abstracting and indexing services relevant to the subject. The list is not restricted to UK publications but includes those from other countries, for example, France and the USA. This is followed by details of current awareness services in the field. Next come details of any published lists of periodicals, followed by a list of libraries visited during the compilation of this part of the directory. The latter list can be used to identify centres of excellence for a particular subject.

The main periodical listing in each section is further subdivided by subject. For example, Section 1 – Philosophy and psychology – includes the following subjects: dowsing, astrology, spiritualism, psychology, sensation, humanism and others. Each entry contains the following information:

UDC classification code
Title, date publication began, frequency, cost
Publisher, publisher's address and telephone number, editor
Contents of a named issue
Additional details, for example previous title, special features.

Subject coverage includes traditional academic journals and 'alternative journals', which makes this directory a useful source book.

The directory contains an index compiled by K. G. B. Bakewell, containing entries under title, subject and sponsoring corporate body. To find periodicals on alternative therapy it is necessary to search through the appropriate subject sections and it can be easy to miss sections – yoga is found under 'religion'.

Whole Again Resource Guide, 1986/87 edn. By Tim Ryan, Patricia J. Case and others (Santa Barbara, CA: SourceNet, 1986).

This book provides an annotated guide to periodicals, directories and other sourcebooks. See entry in the section on 'Directories'.

Willings Press Guide (East Grinstead, Sussex: Skinner). Annual.
This is an international guide to newspapers and periodicals. Coverage is traditional.

Periodicals which contain news and reviews of periodicals

Periodicals are published which announce and review materials from both traditional and alternative publishers. These periodicals can be used to identify new periodicals, changes in periodical titles and so on. In the USA there are many such journals or newsletters, and a selection is listed below. In the UK there is only one main source of this type of information, *The Radical Bookseller*.

Alternative Media. Edited by R. Smith (New York: Alternative Press Syndicate). Biannual.
This is a trade journal for alternative presses in the USA.

Connexions. Edited by Ulli Diemer (Toronto: Connexions). Quarterly.
This is a Canadian alternative press review journal. Each issue concentrates on one topic such as health, food, human rights, and also contains about sixty book and periodical reviews. It also contains annotated listings for groups.

Feminist Bookstore News. Edited by Carol Seajay (San Francisco: FBN). Bi-monthly.
This journal is compiled and edited by Carol Seajay and it is produced bimonthly. The contact address is – 1009 Valencia Street, San Francisco, CA 94110. It has been described as a working tool among feminist bookstores and it contains annotated announcements of works from feminist, small and commercial presses.

New Pages: News and Reviews of the Progressive Book Trade (Grand Blanc: New Pages Press).
This journal is published by the New Pages Press (4426 S. Belsay Road, Grand Blanc, MI 48439). It is aimed at the trade and provides features on the book trade, bookstores and libraries. It includes numerous bibliographies and directories as well as in-depth critical reviews.

The Radical Bookseller (London: Radical Bookseller). Irregular.
This is produced every six to eight weeks by a collective based at 265 Seven Sisters Road, London N4 2DE. It contains news of radical/alternative booksellers and an annotated listing of new books, pamphlets and journals. It is an important source of information on the alternative press in the United Kingdom.

Sirapu (Winters, CA: Sirapu). Biannual.
This journal is published twice a year by Sirapu (Route 1, Box 216, Winters, CA 95694). It is written and published by Noel Peattle and is concerned with alternative librarianship. It provides a useful source of announcements of new publications.

Small Press News. Edited by Diane Kruchkow (New Sharon, ME: Stony Hills, 1981–). Ten issues a year.
Produced ten times a year, this newsletter contains details of small press associations, organizations and events. It announces publications and provides details of conferences and bookfairs.

Small Press Review (Paradise, CA: Dustbooks, 1967–). Monthly.
This monthly journal is produced by Dustbooks (Box 100, Paradise, CA 95969). It is produced on newsprint and contains information about the activities of small presses, new publications and related activities.

The Workbook. Edited by Julie Jacoby (Albuquerque: Southwest Research and Information Center, 1974–). Quarterly.
This periodical reviews alternative and commercial presses, and also government presses which address themes such as health issues.

Tracing periodicals

There is not yet an international source for tracing a specific journal to a location so that the user may consult it. There are national sources which will help. In this section, the national sources in the UK are looked at.

British Union Catalogue of Periodicals (London: Butterworths, 1955–1982).
BUCOP provides a record of periodicals held in British libraries and was produced from information received from the libraries.

Entries are arranged in alphabetical order by journal title, and library location(s) are given for each entry. Despite its age, this is still a very useful tool but it is worth checking with the identified library that it does still hold the journal before visiting.

Current Serials Received (Boston Spa, W Yorks: British Library, 1984).
This is an important source of information for anyone searching for a particular periodical. It lists all the periodicals received at the British Library Document Supply Centre. There are more than 56 000 titles listed in title order. This is a very easy source to use. These items can be borrowed by the inter-library loan facility available at most libraries (if your library doesn't advertise this service ask for further information at the enquiry/information point).

Directory of British Alternative Periodicals, 1965–1974. Edited by J. Noyce (Hassocks, Sussex: Harvester, 1979).
Though dated this directory does contain details of some library holdings.

Keyword Index to Serial Titles (KIST) (Boston Spa, W Yorks: British Library, 1982).
This is a listing of the British Library's (Document Supply Centre and Science Reference Library) master files of periodical titles. It is a keyword index, that is, keywords from the titles are listed in alphabetical order followed by the full title. It can be used to locate a particular title or to verify a title.

Serials in the British Library (London: British Library, 1984).
This publication, which is available on microfiche, lists only new titles received in more than twenty libraries, for example the British Library Science Reference Library, University of Dublin Library and the National Library of Scotland. It can be used as a finding guide but it is important to remember that it reflects only new periodical holdings.

One disadvantage of the sources given above is that many alternative publications are not taken by 'traditional' libraries and so cannot be tracked down using those sources. It is sometimes necessary to write to the publisher and ask for back copies of the items you require. Include enough money to pay for the cost of the journal and postage and packaging.

General therapy periodicals

Examples given in this section are all published in the United Kingdom.

Cahoots (Manchester: Cahoots). Quarterly.
This quarterly publication is described as the North West guide to alternatives and can be contacted at 163 Palestine Road, Manchester, M20 8GH (Tel: 061-445 1568). Contents frequently include articles on different aspects of alternative therapy and also book reviews. There is a calendar where entries are classified into the categories used in the directory: body and mind; centres and communities; creativity and fun; meditation and philosophy; personal growth; social information. This magazine is an essential information source for people living in both the North East and North West of England where it can be obtained from alternative food and bookshops, or on subscription.

Communications (London: MENCAP). Three issues a year.
This information pack contains details of recent reports and articles, news and, occasionally, free copies of government and voluntary body leaflets. It sometimes contains information relevant to alternative therapy.

Creative Mind (Liverpool: Creative Mind). Bi-monthly.
This magazine is produced approximately bi-monthly by a group in Merseyside who can be contacted at *Creative Mind*, Lark Lane Community Association, Lark Lane, Liverpool L17 BUU (Tel: 051–727 8293). It contains articles on many aspects of alternative living and also book reviews. The alternative directory is not restricted to activities in Merseyside, and relevant section headings include bookshops, health, spiritual awareness and social change. It can be obtained from alternative bookshops or on subscription.

Here's Health. Edited by Sarah Bounds (West Byfleet, Surrey: Argus Publications). Monthly.
This monthly publication is published by Argus Health Publications

97

and is available at major newsagents in the UK. It incorporates *New Health*. The magazine includes articles on food and nutrition, natural health (which includes alternative therapy, for example the June 1987 issue includes an article on voice therapy) and other topics such as pollution, gardening and so on. There are about twenty pages of advertisements with entries under many headings including acupuncture, allergies, Alexander technique, aromatherapy, associations, colour healing, counselling, courses, gem elixirs, healing, homeopathy, hypnotherapy, iridology, massage, meditation, polarity therapy, osteopathy, psychic consultants, psychotherapy, reflexology, relaxation, spiritual healing, yoga. A large section is devoted to practitioners' advertisements.

Human Potential (London: HPR, 1977–). Quarterly.
This quarterly publication was established in 1977 as *Human Potential Resources* and changed its title in the summer of 1987. It is published by HPR of 35 Station Road, Hendon, London NW4 4PN (Tel: 01–202 4941). It is available on subscription or from specialist bookshops. It describes itself as a directory, information service and guide covering that broad spectrum of activity that is called the Human Potential Movement. Its contents include papers on various aspects of therapy and personal growth – generally personal accounts; book reviews; resource directory which is divided into sections – counselling/therapy, education, health/healing, spiritual/esoteric, general (which includes holiday centres and bookshops). The range of advertisements in this publication is generally different from that in *Here's Health* and it includes many of the newer kinds of alternative therapies and news of visits to the UK by people who generally work in other countries – particularly the USA.

Link Up (Blockley, Glos: Link up). Quarterly.
This magazine has a global perspective and covers a range of topics which includes alternative therapies. There is a detailed diary of forthcoming events in the UK and a wide range of practitioners and therapy centres advertise in this publication. At irregular intervals it publishes a diary of natural health centres.

New Society (London: New Society). Weekly.
This weekly magazine sometimes contains articles on alternative therapy. It contains details of new publications and forthcoming

short courses. The advertisements sometimes include employment opportunities for alternative therapists, and news of conferences.

One Earth (Forres: Findhorn Foundation). Quarterly.
This magazine is produced by the Findhorn Foundation which is a spiritual and educational body. It is produced quarterly and includes articles on many different aspects of alternative living, for example the Winter 1987 issue contains papers presented at a Spirit of Healing conference held at Findhorn in April 1987. There is a small calendar of events which includes not only those taking place at Findhorn but also workshops and conferences held in the UK and other countries.

Open Mind (London: MENCAP). Bi-monthly.
This is an important journal in the field of mental health and it contains original articles, news, benefits information, letters, book reviews and listings. It sometimes has items on alternative therapy.

Out from the Core. Edited by Nick Totten (Leeds: Self-published, 1986–). Irregular.
This magazine covers many different aspects of radical healing and contains articles from a wide variety of sources. It has resources and contacts sections. It is available in alternative bookshops in the UK or from the author at 23 Knowle Road, Burley, Leeds.

Resurgence (Bideford, Devon: Resurgence). Bi-monthly.
This bi-monthly publication incorporates *Undercurrents,* and can be contacted at Ford House, Hartland, Bideford, Devon. It is available at leading newsagents. The journal includes articles on many aspects of alternative living – education, health, politics, spirituality. Its small ads include entries for alternative therapy workshops, courses and holidays, and also bookshops.

Self Health (London: College of Health). Quarterly.
This is a useful journal which includes original articles, news, alternative medicine round-up, reviews and letters. Its coverage includes alternative therapies.

Spare Rib (London: Spare Rib). Monthly.
A monthly alternative magazine for women, *Spare Rib* is produced collectively and has occasional articles on alternative therapy as well as advertisements for women's therapy. It is available from

leading newsagents and the contact address is 27 Clerkenwell Close, London EC1 0AT.

Official publications

Official publications are those of government bodies, their agencies, and non-government organizations such as the World Health Organization. These bodies sometimes publish items of interest to alternative therapists: examples include reports of investigations into alternative therapy and legislation regarding the legal status of practitioners:

Alternatieve Geneeswijzen in Nederland (*Alternative Systems of Medicine in the Netherlands*). *Report submitted to the State Secretary for Health and Environmental Protection.* Commission for Alternative Systems of Medicine (The Hague: State Publishing Co, 1981).
Legislation and Administrative Regulations on the Use by Licensed Health Services Personnel of Non-Conventional Methods of Diagnosis and Treatment of Illness. Council of Europe (Strasbourg: Council of Europe, 1984).

Government and official publications are traditionally difficult to identify, track down and obtain. However, the libraries and information services within these organizations can be used to help identify and locate particular items. In the United Kingdom the government libraries and information units are described in:

Directory of British Official Publications, 2nd edn. Compiled by Stephen Richard (London: Mansell, 1982).
Although this publication is chiefly concerned with the publications of government organizations it does list over 1300 bodies. It provides addresses, telephone numbers and contacts, and it has useful organizations and subject indexes.

Guide to Government Departments and other Libraries and Information Bureaux (London: British Library Science Reference Library, 1984).
This guide is well presented and divided into sections, that labelled psychology and psychiatry being of most interest to alternative therapists. The detailed entries give the following information: name; address; telephone number; telex number; names and

positions of staff; stock and subject coverage; availability; opening hours; services; and publications.

Information on government libraries and information services in the USA can be obtained from the following publications:

Federal Library Resources: A User's Guide to Research Collections. By Mildred Benton (New York: Science Associates International). *Roster of Federal Libraries: Agency, Geographic, Subject.* By Mildred Benton (Arlington, Virginia: ERIC).

Many countries now produce guides to the library and information services of government bodies and agencies and these can be used to help track down relevant libraries and information units.

Bibliographies, catalogues and sales lists are frequently produced by government bodies and agencies to help distribute their publications. Principal examples include:

Catalogue of British Official Publications not Published by HMSO (Cambridge: Chadwyck-Healey, 1981–).
Government Publications (London: HMSO, 1922–).
Monthly Catalogue of United States Government Publications (Washington, DC: GPO, 1951–).
Sessional Indexes to Parliamentary Papers (London: HMSO, 1828–).

There are many other examples and they can be tracked down using tools such as Walford's *Guide to Reference Materials,* which provides details of catalogues and publications from other government bodies and international organizations.

Research publications

Research into alternative therapy is sometimes carried out in academic organizations and may be published as a thesis or dissertation (the two terms are interchangeable) or as a conference proceeding. These can be a useful information source as they contain both a detailed literature review and a detailed account of original research on a narrow topic. However, they tend to be very academic in their approach. An example of a dissertation is:

An Investigation of the Psycho-Spiritual Dynamics of Hatha Yoga as Contrasted with Western Body Work Therapies (Ph.D. dissertation). By Judith Hanson Lasater (California: California Institute of Asian Studies, 1979).

The main source for British theses is the British Library Document Supply Centre while many North American theses can be obtained from University Microfilms International Dissertations Copies. A useful guide to the availability of theses is:

Guide to the Availability of Theses. Compiled by D. H. Borchadt and J. D. Thawley (Munich: Saur, 1981).

Individual dissertations or theses can be tracked down using printed sources such as:

American Doctoral Dissertations (Ann Arbor, MI: University Microfilms International, 1964–).
This is an annual publication which aims to give a complete listing of all doctoral dissertations accepted by American and Canadian universities and so it includes materials omitted in *Dissertation Abstracts International.*

British Reports, Translations and Theses Received by the British Library Document Supply Centre (Boston Spa: BLDSC, 1981–). Monthly.
This was previously called *BLLD Announcement Bulletin.* Entries are arranged in subject order and it is necessary to browse through a number of sections to find any entries on alternative therapy. There is a keyword index with quarterly and annual indexes. This is a useful source as it also covers the grey literature – semi-published materials.

Comprehensive Dissertation Index, 37 volumes (Ann Arbor, MI: University Microfilms International, 1973).
Covers US doctoral dissertations over the period 1861–1972.

Dissertation Abstracts International (Ann Arbor, MI: University Microfilms International, 1969–).
This is now published in sections: A–Humanities and social sciences; B–Sciences and engineering; C–European abstracts. Sections A and B are produced monthly while C appears quarterly. Entries are arranged under very broad subject headings and there are keyword title and author indexes.

A Guide to Theses and Dissertations: An Annotated International Bibliography of Bibliographies. By M. M. Reynolds (Detroit: Gale, 1975).
This valuable work identifies and annotates about 2500 bibliographies of US and foreign theses and dissertations. Entries are arranged in subject order and there are detailed indexes.

Index to Theses Accepted for Higher Degrees by the Universities of Great Britain and Ireland and by the Council for National Academic Awards (London: ASLIB, 1952–). Biannual.
Each annual index contains over 8000 entries and there are author and subject indexes. This source is also available on magnetic tape from Learned Information, Oxford.

Retrospective Index to Theses of Great Britain and Ireland, 1716–1950. Edited by R. R. Biblboul and F. L. Kent. (Oxford: ABC-Clio, 1975–1977).
This is in five volumes, two of which are likely to be of interest to anyone searching for information on alternative therapy and related subjects: Vol. 1 Social sciences and humanities; Vol. 2 Applied sciences and technology.

Computerized equivalents include the databases:

Dissertation Abstracts Online
SIGLE

AUDIOVISUAL MATERIALS

There is a wide variety of good quality audiovisual materials which can be used by therapists, and particularly by teachers and trainers in this field. A useful guide to audiovisual materials is:

International Guide to Locating Audio-Visual Materials in the Health Sciences. By Margaret C. Jones (Aldershot: Gower, 1986).
The term 'health sciences' is defined very broadly in this book which covers alternative therapies. Part 1 is concerned with finding audiovisual media in the UK, Part 2 with the USA and Canada, and the 'rest of the world' is covered in Part 3. The rest of the book covers selection aids, manual searches, bibliographic guides, and a glossary. There are detailed indexes – general, subject,

country, titles, people. This is a valuable resource to anyone searching for audiovisual media.

This section is divided according to the type of material:

Films and videos
Audio cassettes.

Films and videos

In the UK there are a number of key organizations providing useful publications which can be used to find films and videos relevant to the field of alternative therapy:

BRITISH FILM INSTITUTE, 81 Dean Street, London W1V 6AA
Tel: 01–437 4355
This body produces a number of publications:

British Film Institute and Television Yearbook.
This book lists production companies, exhibitions and distribution organizers. It also gives general information on the film industry and on the BFI.

Film and Video Library Catalogue.
This lists all films, videos and television material available from the BFI library.

British National Film Catalogue.
This is a serial publication which is issued quarterly with annual cumulations. It attempts to cover all films and videos which may be screened to non-fee paying audiences in the UK.

BRITISH UNIVERSITIES FILM AND VIDEO COUNCIL (BUFVC), 55 Greek Street, London W1V 5LR Tel: 01-734 3687
This body provides an information service, an audiovisual reference centre and a higher education film and video library. The following publications may be of use in locating films and videos:

Audio-Visual Materials for Higher Education (AVMHE).
A catalogue which contains a listing of materials used by teachers involved in university-level work.

Higher Education Film and Video Library.
This catalogue contains lists and summaries of films contained in the BUFVC library.

HELPIS (Higher education learning programmes information service).
This catalogue contains details of audiovisual materials that are produced and used by teachers and are available for hire, sale or free loan.

BUFVC Newsletter.
This is published three times a year and it includes details of new audiovisual materials, reviews, details of conferences and so on.

BUFVC Catalogue.
This contains details of films and videos contained in the AVMHE and HELPIS catalogues. Topics include those related to alternative therapy, for example hypnotherapy, behaviour therapy and higher mental processes. It is available on microfiche and as an on-line database.

MENTAL HEALTH FILM COUNCIL, 22 Harley Street, London W1N 2ED Tel: 01-637 0741
MHFC is an educational charity whose aim is to promote the making and use of films in mental health training and education. It organizes film forums and workshops, provides an information service (subscription) and publishes:

MHFC Catalogue.
This catalogue contains many entries relevant to therapists.

MHVC Quarterly Newsletter.

BRITISH ASSOCIATION OF COUNSELLING, 37a Sheep Street, Rugby, Warwickshire CV21 3BX Tel: (0788) 78328
The Association provides a film and video library.

Other organizations

BRITISH LIFE ASSURANCE TRUST (BLAT), BLAT Centre for Health and Medical Education, BMA House, Tavistock Square, London WC1 H9JP Tel: 01-388 7976

105

Provides a variety of services. Main subject area is medicine. Produces a variety of publications and catalogues.

BROADCASTING SUPPORT SERVICES, Room 17, 252 Western Avenue, London W3 6XJ Tel: 01–992 5522
Provides follow-up services for programmes on BBC, Channel 4 and ITV. It publishes viewers' guides and organizes telephone help lines and letter answering services.

GUILD ORGANIZATION LTD, Oundle Road, Peterborough PE2 GP2 Tel: 0733 63122
Distributes and produces films for education, training and commercial markets. Produces a variety of catalogues.

Additional sources

Alternative Views Program Catalog (Austin, TX: Alternative Views, 1983).
This is an annotated listing of over 150 television programmes on alternative topics.

Bullfrog Films (Oley, PA: Bullfrog Films). Biannual.
This is an annotated listing of ninety-four films and tapes about saner living on planet earth.

New Day Film Co-op (Franklin Lakes, NJ: New Day Film Co-op). Annual.
Many of the films in this catalogue reflect the process of life and social changes. There are subject and title indexes.

New Dimensions Radio Catalog (San Fransisco: New Dimensions Foundation, 1982).
This mail order catalogue sells cassette tapes of programmes and interviews with new age people (including therapists).

Psychological Film Register; Films and Videos in the Behavioural Sciences (Pennsylvania: State University, Audiovisual Services, 1944–).
Wishing Well Video Catalog (Graton, CA: Wishing Well Distributing Co). Annual.
This catalogue covers hundreds of alternative videotapes.

Film and video distributors

A variety of sources list film and video distributors, one example being:

Teaching Psychology. Information and Resources. By David Rose and John Radford (London: British Psychological Society, 1984).

Important distributors in the field of alternative therapy include:

CONCORD FILM COUNCIL LTD, 201 Felixstowe Road, Ipswich, Suffolk IP3 9B7 Tel: (0473) 76012
This is a charitable body which distributes films for over 350 other bodies, for example MHFC and Tavistock Clinic. It produces a catalogue which contains descriptions of over 3000 films and videos.

OPEN UNIVERSITY EDUCATIONAL ENTERPRISES LTD, 12 Cofferidge Close, Stony Stratford, Milton Keynes MK11 1BY Tel: (0908) 566744
The OUEE produces a variety of films and videos. These are available through Guild Organization but films for purchase are available from the OUEE.

TAVISTOCK PUBLICATIONS, Associated Book Publishers (UK) Ltd, North Way, Andover, Hants SP10 58R
This organization provides video cassettes which deal with issues relevant to therapists. Titles include *Conversational Model of Psychotherapy* and *Developing a Therapeutic Conversation.*

Audio cassettes

Education cassettes

These are available from a number of bodies including:

British Association for Counselling
Open University Education Enterprises Ltd

They are also available from individuals and organizations such as therapy centres.

Therapeutic cassettes

These can be obtained from a number of sources including:

ALEPH ONE LTD, Old Court House, High Street, Bottisham, Cambridge CB5 9BA Tel: (0223) 811679
This organization produces cassettes in a *Lifestyle Training Centre* series by Robert Sharpe, which use relaxation and stress management techniques.

INSTITUTE OF BEHAVIOUR THERAPY, Life Skill Cassettes, 3 Brighton Road, London EC1V 1LT Tel: 01–837 3500
Produces a series of cassettes by Robert Sharpe which cover stress management.

NEW WORLD CASSETTES, Strawberry Vale, Twickenham TW1 1BR Tel: 01–892 3839
Distributes a variety of cassettes which are appropriate for meditation, relaxation and healing work. Astral music and subliminal tapes are also available.

THORSONS PUBLISHING GROUP, Denington Estate, Wellingborough, Northants NN8 2RQ Tel: (0933) 72525
Distributes a variety of cassettes which are appropriate for meditation, relaxation and healing work.

See also British Film Institute and Concord Film Council.

In the USA the following organizations produce and/or distribute cassettes:

CENTRE FOR APPLIED INTUITION, 2046 Clement Street, San Francisco, CA 94121
This organization produces and distributes cassettes of its conferences and lectures. These include recorded trance channelling sessions.

POTENTIALS UNLIMITED, 4804H Broadmoor SE, Grand Rapids, MI 49508

Distributes cassettes on a variety of subjects including hypnosis. This company also produces a free catalogue.

SOURCE CASSETTES, Dept M176, PO Box W, Stanford CA 94305
Distributes a variety of cassettes including the classics, *The Healing Journey* and *Letting Go of Stress*, by Emmett E. Miller.

TOOLS FOR CHANGE, PO Box 14141,San Fransisco, CA 94114
Produces and distributes tapes on meditation, guided visualizations for people with AIDS.

VALLEY OF THE SUN PUBLISHING, Box 38, Malibu, CA 90265
Produces a catalogue of its subliminal tapes which include *Stress Control, Healing Acceleration* and *Psychic Ability*.

WESTWOOD PUBLISHING COMPANY, 312 Riverdale Drive, Glendale, CA 91204
The company's mail order catalogue *Hypnotism and Mind Power Books & Cassettes* describes books and cassettes on hypnotism, hypnotherapy, meditation and stress reduction.

YES! BOOKSHOP, 1035 31st St NW, Washington DC 20007
Cris Popenoe edited this bookshop catalogue *Records and Cassettes: A Selected Guide,* which was produced in 1983. This catalogue is extensive and covers cassettes for health and healing; meditation; past lives; relaxation; sleep and dreams; stress control; visualization; yoga; body movement. It also includes choral music, non-Western music, new age music, electronic music and the sounds of nature.

COMPUTERIZED INFORMATION SOURCES

This section covers printed guides to computerized information searching; directories or guides to on-line databases; a selected list of databases; CD-ROM; videotex; and a brief resumé of other computerized sources.

109

Guides to computerized information searching

Computerized information searching (or on-line searching) can be an expensive process which requires skilled searchers. The following books provide a good introduction to the subject:

Computerized Literature Searching: Research Strategies and Databases. By C. L. Gilreath (Boulder, CO: Westview, 1984).
A readable book which provides a good general introduction.

Online Bibliographic Databases, 4th edn. By J. L. Hall and M. J. Brown (London: ASLIB, 1986).
Online Searching: An Introduction. By W. M. Henry, J. A. Leigh, L. A. Tedd and others (London: Butterworths, 1980).

On-line databases

Thousands of databases are now available throughout the world. While many are unlikely to contain references of interest to alternative therapists some will contain useful materials. Helpful guides to databases include:

Accessible Databases: A Directory of Online and Machine-Readable Information Sources. Edited by Douglas Tookey (London: Spiegler and Pegler, 1987).
This directory is international in coverage and covers almost 800 databases. For each database, information is presented under the following headings:

Database details: type; subject; geographic coverage; content size; timespan; updating frequency; source; owner; number of users.
Access restrictions; method; terminals; vendors; costs; other information.

This source includes the following indexes: abbreviated names index; vendors index; owners, IPs index; subject index.

Database Directory (White Plains, NY: Knowledge Industry). Annual.
This directory is available on-line under the same name. It covers more than 1800 databases available in North America. There are subject, producer and vendor indexes.

Directory of Online Databases (Santa Monica: Cuadra, 1979-). Annual.
This quarterly directory consists of two directory issues and two updates. It covers more than 2600 databases and contains detailed information about each database. It is fully indexed and is available on-line as Cuadra Directory of Databases.

Inventory of Abstracting and Indexing Services Produced in the UK. By J. Stephens (London: British Library, 1986).
This directory provides information on 430 databases produced in the UK. It covers both on-line and printed databases and provides a wealth of information about these sources.

Databases

A large number of databases are likely to be of interest to searchers tor information on alternative therapies. They are listed below under the following subject headings:

Books
Conferences/papers/proceedings
Education
Health care
Information services
Multidisciplinary
News/newspapers
Official publications
Organizations
Periodicals
Psychology
Religious studies
Social sciences
Theses

Books

Book Review Digest
Book Review Index
Books in Print
Booksinfo

Cumulative Book Index
LC/MARC (UK) or LC/LINE (USA and Canada)
Superindex (back of book indexes)
UK MARC
Whitaker
Wiley Catalog/Online

Conferences/papers/proceedings

Conf
Conference Papers Index
Conference Proceedings Index
SIGLE

Education

British Education Index
Education Index
ERIC
Language and Language Behaviour Abs

Health care

British Medical Association Press Cuttings
CHID (Combined health information database)
EMBASE (*Excerpta Medica*)
Heclinet
Medline
Mental Health Abstracts
Nursing and Allied Health
Pre-med

Information services

Cuadra Directory of Databases
Database of Databases

Multidisciplinary

Abstrax 400 (popular US periodicals)
Bibliographic Index
Magazine asap/index (popular US)

News/newspapers

National Newspaper Index (US)
NDEX (Newspaper Index – chiefly US)
Newsearch (US – current awareness)
UPI news (United Press index)
Washington Post Index
World Reporter

Official publications

Acompline
DHSS-DATA
Federal Index
Federal Register Abstracts
GPO Monthly Catalog
GPO Publications Reference File
Polis

Organizations

Associations Publications in Print
Electronic Yellow Pages
Encyclopedia of Associations

Periodicals

California Union List of Periodicals
Journal Directory
Reader's Guide to Periodicals
Ulrich's International Periodicals Directory

Psychology

National Clearing House for Mental Health
Psycalert
Psycinfo
Psyn

Religious studies

Religion Index

Social sciences

Social scisearch
Social work abstracts
Sociological abstracts

Theses

Dissertations abstracts online
SIGLE

CD-ROM

Copies of databases are becoming increasingly available in CD-ROM format. Current examples include:

A-V online
A database of audiovisual materials from the US National Information Center for Educational Media (NICEM). It covers the complete database and is updated annually.

ERIC
A bibliographic database sponsored by the US Department of Education which consists of resources in education (RIE) file, and the current index to journals in education (CIJE) file.

There are also:

Medline
Psyclit
Sociofile

A new guide to CD-ROM products is:

CD-ROM Directory 1988 (London: TFPL, 1987).
This directory lists products available on CD-ROM. Each entry contains the following details: name of product; vendor; information provider; information type; when the product first appeared; frequency of update; stage of development; general configuration; recommended hardware; specific software; price; brief description of subject coverage.

The directory also contains details of company information, books, journals, conferences and exhibitions. It is fully indexed.

Videotex

Some information on the alternative therapies is available on view-data systems. For example, the British Prestel system contains some information on some alternative therapies. To date there are no comprehensive information services on this subject available in this format.

Other sources

There are many other computerized information sources which may contain items of interest to anyone searching for information on alternative therapy. For example, in the UK many polytechnics and universities have computerized library catalogues (on-line public access catalogues – or OPACs) and it is possible to access these via a computer network called JANET. So, someone at Leeds Polytechnic using the polytechnic's PRIME computer system could access via JANET an on-line catalogue of, say, a university in Scotland and find out whether or not its collection included books on a particular aspect of therapy.

A more specific example is that of the computerized database maintained by the Yoga Biomedical Trust (PO Box 140, Cambridge CB1 1PU, UK) which contains more than 1500 references on yoga research. The Trust produces a printed publication, *Bibliography of Research Literature on Yoga,* with periodic updates. This bibliography is also available on floppy disc.

Another specialized database is held at Hertfordshire College (7

Hatfield Road, St Albans AL1 3RS) and it covers arts and psychology. This database contains items relating to arts, disability and therapy throughout the European Community. Sue Ball is the European Project Leader.

6

Specialized sources: acupressure to crystal healing

ACUPRESSURE

Acupressure is believed to have originated in China as a form of needleless acupuncture for first-aid and self-help purposes. It is also practised under the name of G-Jo and in the Japanese form of Shiatsu (see Chapter 8). Acupressure involves applying pressure and massaging points on the acupuncture meridians to correct the flow of Ch'i or energy and so help the person to achieve wholeness and a balanced state. While acupressure can be used to help physical ailments, it can also be used to help an individual achieve psychological growth and balance.

Resources

REFERENCE ITEMS

Mind-Body Therapies. A Select Bibliography of Books in English. Compiled by Robin Monro, Joanna E. Trevelyan and Ruth West (London: Mansell, 1987).
This bibliography has a section on acupressure and Shiatsu which contains approximately sixty-seven references.

BOOKS

Bahr, F. R. (1982) *The Acupressure Health Book,* Unwin, London.
Blate, M. (1982) *Advanced G-Jo: The Natural Healer's Acupressure Handbook,* Routledge and Kegan Paul, London.
Blate, M. (1978) *The Natural Healers' Acupressure Handbook,* Routledge and Kegan Paul, London.
Ewald, H. (1978) *Acupressure Techniques,* Thorsons, Wellingborough.
Houston, F. M. (1974) *The Healing Benefits of Acupressure: Acupuncture Without Needles,* Keats, New Canaan, CONN.
Kenyon, J. N. (1987) *Self Help Acupressure Techniques: Home Treatment for a Wide Number of Conditions,* Thorsons, Wellingborough.
Kenyon, K. (1974) *Pressure Points: Do It Yourself Acupuncture Without Needles,* Acro, New York.
Lavier, J. (1977) *Chinese Micro-Massage: Acupuncture Without Needles,* Thorsons, Wellingborough.
Manaka, Y. and Urquart, I. (1983) *Quick and Easy Chinese Massage,* Shufunotomo, Japan.
Shiffrin, N. (1976) *Acupressure,* Major Books, Canoga Park, California.
Taylor, L. and Bryant, B. (1984) *Acupressure Yoga and You,* Japan Publications, Tokyo.
Warren, F. Z. (1976) *Freedom from Pain Through Acupressure,* Wentworth, New York.

ALEXANDER TECHNIQUE

The Alexander technique is often described as a form of education rather than a therapy. It is a technique which works at the level of posture to help change and correct bad habits. As a result, the body is taught to follow a more balanced and correct pattern of use. This change at a postural level may then be followed by changes at a psychological or spiritual level.

Resources

REFERENCE ITEMS

Mind-Body Therapies. A Select Bibliography of Books in English, Compiled by Robin Monro, Joanna E. Trevelyan and Ruth West (London: Mansell, 1987).
This bibliography has a section on the Alexander technique which contains approximately seventeen references.

PERIODICALS

The Alexander Journal (London: Society of Teachers of the Alexander Technique).

BOOKS

Alexander, F. M. (1929) *Constructive Conscious Control of the Individual,* Methuen, London.
Alexander, F. M. (1942) *The Universal Constant in Living,* Chaterson, London.
Alexander, F. M. (1945) *Man's Supreme Inheritance: Conscious Guidance and Control in Relation to Human Evolution in Civilisation,* Integral Press, Bexley Heath, Kent.
Alexander, F. M. (1971) *The Resurrection of the Body,* Dell, New York.
Alexander, F. M. (1985) *The Use of the Self,* Gollancz, London. Originally published 1932.
Barker, S. (1978) *The Alexander Technique: The Revolutionary Way to Use Your Body for Total Energy,* Bantam, Toronto; London.
Barlow, W. (1980) *The Alexander Technique,* Arrow, London.
Barlow, W. (1981) *The Alexander Principle,* Arrow, London.
Byles, M. (1978) *Stand Straight Without Strain: The Original Exercises of F. Matthias Alexander,* Fowler, London.
Gelb, M. (1981) *Body Learning: An Introduction to the Alexander Technique,* Delilah Books, New York.
Jones, F. P. (1976) *Body Awareness in Action,* Wildwood, Aldershot.

Maisel, E. (1974) *The Alexander Technique: The Essential Writings of F. Matthias Alexander,* Thames and Hudson, London.
Stevens, C. *Alternative health. Alexander technique,* Futura, London.
Stransky, J. with Stone, R. (c1981) *The Alexander Technique: Joy in the Life of Your Body,* Beaufort, New York.

Organizations

ALEXANDER TEACHING ASSOCIATES, ATA Centre, 188 Old Street, London EC1V 9BP Tel: 01-250 3038

THE SOCIETY OF TEACHERS OF THE ALEXANDER TECHNIQUE, 3b Albert Court, Kensington Gore, London SW7 Tel: 01-589 3834

AROMATHERAPY

Aromatherapy is the use of essential oils to promote physical, psychological and spiritual well-being. The essential oils are normally applied externally, frequently as part of a massage. Different oils have different effects: lavender is a balancer; patchouli can be used to help open and balance the sacral chakra; camphor can be used to help head colds.

Resources

REFERENCE ITEMS

Mind-Body Therapies. A Select Bibliography of Books in English, Compiled by Robin Monro, Joanna E. Trevelyan and Ruth West (London: Mansell, 1987).
This bibliography has a section on aromatherapy.

BOOKS

Arnould-Taylor, W. E. (1981) *Aromatherapy for the Whole Person: Physessential Therapy,* Thornes, Cheltenham.

Davis, P. and Stead, C. (1986) *An Aromatherapist's Alphabet,* Daniel, Saffron Waldron, Essex.

Genders, R. (1977) *A Book of Aromatics,* Darton, Longman and Todd, London.

Genders, R. (1978) *Scented Flora of the World: An Encyclopedia,* Mayflower, London.

Jackson, J. (1984) *Aromatherapy,* Dorling Kindersley, London.

Lautie, R. and Passebecq, A. (1984) *Aromatherapy: The Use of Plant Essences in Healing,* Thorsons, Wellingborough.

Price, S. (1983) *Practical Aromatherapy: How to Use Essential Oils to Restore Vitality,* Thorsons, Wellingborough.

Ryman, D. (1984) *The Aromatherapy Book,* Century, London.

Ryman, D. (1986) *The Madame Maury Guide to Aromatherapy,* Daniel, Saffron Waldron, Essex.

Tisserand, R. B. (1977) *The Art of Aromatherapy,* Daniel, London.

Tisserand, R. B. (1985) *The Essential Oil Safety Data Manual,* Association of Aromatherapists, London.

Valnet, J. (1982) *The Practice of Aromatherapy,* translated by R. Campbell and L. Houston, Daniel, London.

ART THERAPY

Art therapy is a form of therapy which uses art, in its widest sense, to help promote change and growth in a person. The techniques used may involve painting or drawing, mask making, collage or model making. Art therapy is frequently used within the health and special education services in the UK and other countries.

Resources

REFERENCE ITEMS

American Art Therapy Association Directory (Reston, VA: American Art Therapy Association, 1979).

121

A geographic listing of art therapists and members.

Art Therapy and Groupwork: An Annotated Bibliography. Edited by K. M. Hanes (Westport, CN: Greenwood, 1982).
Art Therapy Bibliography. 1981 (London: BAAT, 1981).
BAAT Register of Art Therapists (London: BAAT). Annual.
The Creative Tree. Edited by Gina Levete (Wilton, Salisbury: Michael Russell, 1987).
This book has a directory which is international in its coverage and includes organizations, publications, and resources listed under the following headings: arts, community; arts, hospital; arts, visual; craft/craft training schemes, art therapy training courses; organizations for information on art therapy training; general creative therapy training courses.

PERIODICALS

AATA Newsletter. Edited by Barbara Katz Mandel (Reston, VA: American Art Therapy Association). Bi-monthly.
This newsletter provides information about resources, professional opportunities; training courses; and members' activities.

American Journal of Art Therapy (Washington, DC: American Art Therapy Association). Quarterly.
This professional journal contains articles, case studies, reader's forum, news and notes on recent periodicals and book reviews.

The Arts in Psychotherapy (Fayetteville, NJ: ANKHO).

Art Therapy Newsletter (London: BAAT). Quarterly.
This is the newsletter of the BAAT and it contains information about the Association's activities, job vacancies and workshops.

Inscape. Edited by Christine Wood (London: BAAT). Biannual.
This journal contains articles, book reviews and details of the contents of previous back issues.

Spectrum: The Art Magazine for the Physically Handicapped (Epsom, Surrey: Conquest).

BOOKS

Adamson, E. (1984) *Art as Healing,* Coverture, London.

Anderson, W. (Ed) (1977) *Therapy and the Arts: Tools of Consciousness,* Harper and Row, New York.

Betensky, M. (1973) *Self Discovery through Self Expression,* Thomas, Springfield, ILL.

Boos-Hamburger, H. (1973) *The Creative Power of Colour,* Michael Press and Krisha Press, New York.
This book covers Steiner painting techniques.

Burns, R. C. and Kaufman, S. H. (1972) *Actions, Styles and Symbols in Kinetic Family Drawings: An Interpretive Manual,* Constable, London.

Dalley, T. (Ed) (1984) *Art as Therapy: An Introduction to the Use of Art as a Therapeutic Technique,* Tavistock, London.

Dalley, T. (1987) *Images of Art Therapy,* Tavistock, London.

Edwards, B. (1982) *Drawing on the Right Side of the Brain,* Fontana, London.

Edwards, B. (1987) *Drawing on the Artist Within,* Collins, London.
This well-produced book has an extensive bibliography on items concerned with art, consciousness and creativity.

Ehrenzweig, A. (1970) *The Hidden Order of Art,* Prentice-Hall, Englewood Cliffs, NJ.

Feldman, E. B. (1970) *Becoming Human Through Art,* Prentice-Hall, Englewood Cliffs, NJ.

Franck, F. (1974) *The Zen of Seeing,* Wildwood, Aldershot.

Harris, J. and Joseph, C. (1973) *Murals of the Mind,* IUP, New York.

Keyes, M. F. (1974) *The Inward Journey,* Celestial Arts, Millbrae, CA.

Koch, E. and Wagner, G. (1980) *The Individuality of Colour,* Rudolf Steiner Press, Blauvelt, NJ.

Kwiatkowska, H. (1978) *Family Art Therapy,* Thomas, Springfield, IL.

Landgarten, H. B. (1981) *Clinical Art Therapy,* Bruner Mazel, NY.

Liebmann, M. (1986) *Art Therapy for Groups,* Croom Helm, London.
This is a valuable book which can be used as a resource tool for art therapists and art therapy students. Its bias is towards the UK

and it contains useful information on obtaining resources. There is a detailed bibliography.

Luthe, W. (1976) *Creativity Mobilization Technique,* Grune and Stratton, New York.

Naumberg, M. (1966) *Dynamically Oriented Art Therapy,* Grune and Stratton, New York.

Oaklander, V. (1978) *Windows to our Children,* Real People Press, Moab, UT.

Pavey, D. (1979) *Art-Based Games,* Methuen, London.

Rhyne, J. (1984) *The Gestalt Art Experience,* Magnolia Street Publishers, USA.

Robbins, A. (1987) *The Artist as Therapist,* Human Sciences, New York.

Robbins, A. and Sibley, L. B. (1976) *Creative Art Therapy,* Bruner Mazel, New York.

Rubin, J. A. (1984) *The Art of Art Therapy,* Van Nostrand Reinhold, New York.

Ullman, E. and Dachinger, P. (Eds) (1976) *Art Therapy in Theory and Practice,* Schocken, New York.

Ullman, E. and Levy, C. A. (Eds) (1980) *Art Therapy Viewpoints,* Schocken, New York.

Wadeson, H. (1980) *Art Psychotherapy,* Wiley, Chichester.

Warren, B. (Ed) (1984) *Using the Creative Arts in Therapy,* Croom Helm, London.

Weismann, D. L. (1970) *The Visual Arts as Human Experience,* Prentice-Hall, Englewood Cliffs, NJ.

Williams, G. W. and Wood, M. M. (1977) *Developmental Art Therapy,* University Park Press, Baltimore.

FILM AND VIDEO

Art Therapy. Produced by T. Dalley and D. Waller, directed by J. Beacham (London: Tavistock Videotapes, 1984).

Organizations

AMERICAN ART THERAPY ASSOCIATION, 1980 Isaac Newton Square S, Reston, VA 22090 Tel: (703) 370–3223

BRITISH ASSOCIATION OF ART THERAPISTS, C/o 13c Northwood Road, London N6 5TL

INTERNATIONAL SOCIETY FOR ART, CREATION, THERAPY, C/o Abteilung für Arbeits u. Sozialhygiene Klinikum der Universität Heidelberg Im Neuenheimerfeld 368, 6900 Heidelberg 1, West Germany

ASTROLOGICAL COUNSELLING

The central idea of astrology is that the macrocosm (sun, moon and planets) influences individuals and life on earth. Although astrology is found in many guises – from superficial newspaper horoscopes to its use as an aid to employee selection – it is included in this book because many astrologers use their skills alongside counselling and therapeutic techniques to help an individual develop, particularly at a psychological level.

Bookshops

L. N. FOWLER & CO LTD, 1201 High Road, Chadwell Heath, Romford, Essex RM6 4DH Tel: 01-597 2491
Mail order, catalogue available, showroom.

Publishers

CRCS PUBLICATIONS, PO Box 4307, Vancouver, Washington 98662, USA

Resources

REFERENCE ITEMS

Astrology: A Comprehensive Bibliography. By Cris Popenoe (Washington, DC: YES! Bookshop, 1982).
This list covers about 1000 items with full bibliographic citations. There is no index.

The Knot of Time: Astrology and the Female Experience. By Lindsay River and Sally Gillespie (London: The Women's Press, 1987).
Has a very detailed bibliography.

NASO International Astrological Directory. Edited by Barbara Somerfield (New York: National Astrological Directory, 1984).
This directory lists local, national and international astrology societies, research organizations, periodicals and practitioners.

Whole Again Resource Guide, 1986/87. By Tim Ryan and Patricia J. Case (Santa Barbara, CA: SourceNet, 1986).
Has a complete section on astrology with fifty-two references.

PERIODICALS

American Astrology. Edited by Joanne Clancy (New York: Starlog). Monthly.
A popular magazine containing news items, articles, advertisements and day-by-day astrological guidance.

American Federation of Astrologers Bulletin (Tempe, AZ: AFA). Monthly.
A serious journal full of good quality articles.

Astrology. Edited by Barbara Somerfield (New York: National Astrological Society). Quarterly.
A good quality journal.

Astrology. Edited by Geoffrey Cornelius (London: Astrological Lodge). Quarterly.
This publication is associated with the Theosophical Society of England and has a spiritual emphasis.

Australian Astrologers' Journal. Edited by Dymock Broase (Blackheath, NSW: Australian Astrologers' Cooperative). Quarterly.
This is a typed journal with charts.

Horoscope (London: Atlas). Monthly.
Another popular magazine whose contents are similar to those in *American Astrology.*

126

New Astrologer. Edited by Jo Baker (Glastonbury: SB Publications, 1987–).
This is a bi-monthly magazine of the Faculty of Astrological Studies, UK. It includes news items, articles, book reviews and advertisements.

Prediction. Edited by Jo Logan (Croydon, Surrey: Link House). Monthly.
A popular magazine containing news, articles, letters, day-by-day astrological guidance, book reviews and advertisements.

BOOKS

Arroyo, S. (1975) *Astrology, Psychology and the Four Elements,* CRCS Publications, Vancouver.
Arroyo, S. (1978) *Astrology, Karma and Transformations,* CRCS Publications, Vancouver.
Cunningham, D. (1978) *An Astrological Guide to Self-Awareness,* CRCS Publications, Vancouver.
Fenton, S. (1987) *Moon Signs,* Aquarian, Wellingborough.
Gauquelin, M. (1976) *Cosmic Influences on Human Behaviour,* Futura, London.
Greene, L. (1976) *Saturn,* Aquarian, Wellingborough.
Greene, L. (1977) *Relating: An Astrological Guide to Living with Others on a Small Planet,* Coventure, London.
Greene, L. (1983) *The Outer Planets and Their Cycles,* CRCS Publications, Vancouver.
Greene, L. (1984) *The Astrology of Fate,* Allen & Unwin, London.
Greene, L. and Sasportas, H. (1987) *The Development of the Personality. Seminars in Psychological Astrology. Vol. 1,* Routledge & Kegan Paul, London.
Mayo, J. (1964) *Astrology,* Hodder & Stoughton, London.
River, L. and Gillespie, S. (1987) *The Knot of Time: Astrology and the Female Experience,* The Women's Press, London.
Walters, D. (1987) *Chinese Astrology,* Aquarian, Wellingborough.

Multimedia

AFA PRODUCT PRICE LIST, American Federation of Astrologers, PO Box 22040, Tempe, AZ 85282 Tel: (602) 838-1751
The price list includes books, ephemerides, tables of houses, calendars, charts, aids and computer hardware and software.

Computerized sources

There are now many computer programs available for constructing horoscopes with the help of home computers. Some suppliers in the UK are given below; others can be identified using astrological periodicals.

ASTROCALC, 67 Peascroft Road, Hemel Hempstead, Herts HP3 8ER Tel: (0422) 51809

THE ELECTRIC EPHEMERIS, 214 Finchley Road, Hampstead, London NW3 6DH

NEW MOON SOFTWARE, 18 Grafton Road, Harrow, Middlesex HA1 4QT

Organizations

AMERICAN FEDERATION OF ASTROLOGERS, PO Box 22040, Tempe, AZ 85282 Tel: (602) 838-1751

ASTROLOGICAL ASSOCIATION OF GREAT BRITAIN, 2 Waltham Close, Abbey Park, West Bridgford, Nottingham NG2 6LE

AUSTRALIAN ASTROLOGERS' COOPERATIVE, 86 Clarence Road, Blackheath, New South Wales, Australia 2785 Tel: (047) 87-8874

THE COMPANY OF ASTROLOGERS, 6 Queen Square, Bloomsbury, London WC1 3AR Tel: 01–837 4410

NATIONAL ASTROLOGICAL SOCIETY, 205 3rd Avenue, New York, NY 10003 Tel: (212) 673-1831

BODYMIND THERAPIES

The bodymind therapies considered here have developed in a number of ways – from the work of Reich and others, and as a result of synthesis of a number of Eastern and Western approaches. These therapies tend to work at all three levels – physical, emotional and spiritual – to help individuals to grow and change. The following therapies are included in this section:

1 *Bioenergetics* is a bodymind approach which was initially developed by Lowen, a student and client of Reich. Bioenergetics involves the use of massage and special exercises to help release muscle tensions and emotional blocks.
2 *Biodynamic psychology*, developed by Gerda Boyeson, also uses massage and exercises but also psycho-peristaltic regulation.
3 Boadella has developed *biosynthesis*, which uses principles derived from prenatal development and from the work of Reich.
4 *Dreambody theory and practice*, developed by Arnold Mindell, is a synthesis of the work from many schools including that of Jung.
Related subject headings include massage therapy, Reichian therapy, T'ai chi and yoga.

Resources

PERIODICALS

Bio-Energetic Institute Monographs. Written by Alexander Lowen and John Pierrakos (New York: Bio-energetic Institute, 1963–). Annual.
Journal of Biological Experience. Edited by Ian J. Grand (Berkeley, CA: Center for Energetic Studies). Biannual.
This professional journal looks at bioenergetics in its broadest sense.

BOOKS

Boadella, D. (Ed) (1976) *In the Wake of Reich,* Coventure, Denham, Bucks.

Boadella, D. (1987) *Lifestreams: An Introduction to Biosynthesis,* Routledge & Kegan Paul, London.

Boadella, D. (in press) 'Biosynthesis', in J. Rowan (Ed) *Innovative Therapies in Britain,* Open University, Milton Keynes.

Boyeson, G. (1985) *Entre Psyche et Soma,* Payot, Paris.

Dychtwald, K. (1977) *Bodymind,* Wildwood, Aldershot.

Ernst, S. and Goodison, L. (1981) *In Our Own Hands: A Book of Self-Help Therapy,* The Women's Press, London.
Contains a useful section on bodywork which sets bioenergetics in the context of Reichian and other forms of bodywork.

Keleman, S. (1974) *Living Your Dying,* Random House, Westminster, MD.

Keleman, S. (1975) *The Human Ground,* Center Press, Berkeley, CA.

Keleman, S. (1976) *Your Body Speaks its Mind,* Pocket Books, New York.

Keleman, S. (1985) *Emotional Anatomy,* Center Press, Berkeley, CA.

Keleman, S. (1985) *Somatic Reality,* Center Press, Berkeley, CA.

Kurtz, R. and Pretera, H. (1976) *The Body Reveals,* Harper & Row, New York.

Lowen, A. (1958) *Physical Dynamics of Character Structure,* Collier Books, New York. Reprinted as Lowen (1969).

Lowen, A. (1965) *Love and Orgasm,* Macmillan, New York.

Lowen, A. (1969) *The Language of the Body,* Collier, New York. Macmillan, London.

Lowen, A. (1972) *Depression and the Body,* Collier Macmillan, New York.

Lowen, A. (1973) *The Betrayal of the Body,* Collier, New York.

Lowen, A. (1976) *Bioenergetics,* Penguin, Harmondsworth. (Previously published in the USA by Coward, McCann & Geoghegan, 1975.)

Lowen, A. and Lowen, L. (1977) *The Way to Vibrant Health,* Harper & Row, London.

Mindell, A. (1984) *Dreambody. The Body's Role in Revealing the Self,* Routledge & Kegan Paul, London.
Mindell, A. (1985) *River's Way,* Routledge & Kegan Paul, London.
Mindell, A. (1985) *Working with the Dreambody,* Routledge & Kegan Paul, London.
Mindell, A. (1987) *The Dreambody in Relationships,* Routledge & Kegan Paul, London.
Mott, F. (1948) *Bio-synthesis,* David McKay, Philadelphia.

Organizations

CENTRE FOR BIOSYNTHESIS, David Boadella, BCM Chesil, London WC1N 3XX

HAKOMI INSTITUTE, 61 Grantham Road, London W4 2RT
and also at Boulder, Colorado, USA
Hakomi was founded by Ron Kurtz and has its roots in body-centred therapies such as bioenergetics, modern systems theory, and Taoism and Buddhism.

INSTITUTE FOR BIO-ENERGETIC ANALYSIS, Alexander Lowen and John Pierrakos, Director, 71 Park Avenue,New York 16, USA

INSTITUTE FOR BIO-ENERGY, Gerda Boyeson, Director, PO Box 750, London WC1

WESTERN INSTITUTE FOR BIO-ENERGETIC ANALYSIS, Stanley Keleman, Director, 1645 Virginia, Berkeley, California, USA

CO-COUNSELLING

Co-counselling is a method of self-help therapy which involves two trained individuals (the training lasts a minimum of forty hours) giving each other sessions on a 'swops' basis. Co-counselling uses catharsis to help remove blocked emotions. It is very much a client defined therapy with the counsellor often having a minimum role.

Publishers

HUMAN POTENTIAL RESEARCH PROJECT, University of Surrey, Guildford, Surrey GU2 5XH Tel: (0483) 571281

RATIONAL ISLAND PRESS, PO Box 2081, Main Office Station, Seattle Washington 98111, USA

Resources

PERIODICALS

Firelighter. Edited by Rose Evison and Richard Horobin (Sheffield: Co- counselling Phoenix). Irregular.
An occasional publication which contains articles and reviews on all aspects of co-counselling.

Present Time. By Harvey Jackins (Seattle: Rational Island, 1970–). This is the official magazine of the Re-evaluation co-counselling group in the USA. They publish many other specialist magazines:

Black Re-emergence
Classroom
Colleague
The Re-evaluation Counseling Teacher
Sisters
Priests and Nuns Newsletters
Young and Powerful – and many others.

BOOKS

Ernst, S. and Goodison, L. (1981) *In Our Own Hands: A Book of Self-Help Therapy,* Women's Press, London.
Contains a useful section on co-counselling.
Evison, R. and Horobin, R. (1985) *How to Change Yourself and Your World,* 2nd edn. Co-counselling Phoenix, Sheffield.
A very practical and visually interesting manual on co-counselling. It includes a short annotated bibliography.
Jackins, H. (1970) *Fundamentals of Co-counseling Manual,* Rational Island, Seattle.

Jackins, H. (1975) *The Human Side of Human Beings: The Theory of Re-evaluation Counseling,* Rational Island, Seattle.
This is a classic book on co-counselling.
Saunders, L. (Ed) (1987) *Glancing Fires: An Investigation into Women's Creativity,* Women's Press, London.
This book is a series of essays by creative women. Many of them mention co-counselling with respect to the development of their creativity.

PAMPHLETS

Co-counselling. Revised edn by John Heron (Guildford: HPRP, 1979).
Co-counselling: An Experiential Enquiry, 1. By John Heron and Peter Reason (Guildford: HPRP, 1981).
Co-counselling: An Experiential Enquiry, 2. By John Heron and Peter Reason (Guildford: HPRP, 1982).
Co-counselling Teachers Manual. By John Heron (Guildford: HPRP, 1977).
Re-evaluation Counselling: A Theoretical Review. By John Heron (Guildford: HPRP, 1973).

Audiovisual resources

Present Time contains a listing of re-evaluation counselling video cassettes. They include titles such as:

The Human Side of Human Beings: An Introduction to RC
No Limits for Women
Sound Fundamentals and Advanced Progress in Re-evaluation Counselling Theory
Taking Charge No 1-4
Why Women Must Emphasize Women's Issues

These are all available from Rational Island Publishers.

Organizations

CO-COUNSELLING PHOENIX, 5 Victoria Road, Sheffield S10 2DJ Tel: (0742) 686371

RE-EVALUATION COUNSELLING, Rational Island Press, PO Box 2081, Main Office Station, Seattle, Washington 98111, USA Can provide a detailed listing of RC counsellors throughout the world.

COLOUR THERAPY

The use of colour to effect change and healing has been known and practised since ancient times. The use of colour therapy involves using colour at subtle energy levels.

Resources

BOOKS

Anderson, M. (1979) *Colour Healing,* 2nd edn, Aquarian, Wellingborough.
Birren, F. (1941) *The Story of Colour,* Crimson, Westport, CT.
Birren, F. (1950) *Colour Psychology and Colour Healing,* Citadel, Secaucus, NJ.
Gimbel, T. (1980) *Healing Through Colour,* Daniel, Saffron Walden.
Ostrom, J. (1987) *You and Your Aura,* Aquarian, Wellingborough.
Ouseley, S. G. J. (1949) *Colour Meditations,* Fowler, Romford, Essex.
Ouseley, S. G. J. (1951) *The Power of the Rays,* Fowler, Romford, Essex.
Wilson, A. and Bek, L. (1981) *What Colour Are You?,* Aquarian, Wellingborough.
Wood, B. (1981) *The Healing Power of Colour,* Aquarian, Wellingborough.

CRYSTAL HEALING

Crystal healing involves the use of crystals such as amethyst, garnet and obsidian to help balance an individual's energy field. The crystals may be held by the person or placed on particular parts of his or her body. This subject has grown rapidly in the 1970s and 1980s. The use of crystal essences is not covered in this bibliography.

Resources

REFERENCE ITEMS

Crystal Cosmos Network Directory. Edited by Elizabeth Logan (Winnipeg, Man: Crystal Cosmos Network, 1986).
This directory lists over 200 healers who work with crystals. It also includes publishers, networkers and educators.

Gem Elixirs and Vibrational Healing 1 and 2 (see below).
These books contain exhaustive bibliographies.

PERIODICALS

Crystal News, (St Anne's on the Sea, Lancashire: Crystal Research Foundation, 1987–). Bi-monthly.
This magazine contains reports, news and reviews. Coverage is not restricted to the UK.

BOOKS

Alper, F. (1982-1985) *Exploring Atlantis,* Arizona Metaphysical Society, Phoenix.
Bonewitz, R. (1983) *Cosmic Crystals. Crystal Consciousness and the New Age,* Turnstone, Turnstone.
Bonewitz, R. (1986) *The Cosmic Crystal Spiral,* Element Books, Longmead.
Deaver, K. (1985) *Rock Crystal: The Magic Stone,* Weising, York Beach, Maine.
Gurudas (1985) *Gem Elixirs and Vibrational Healing 1,* channeled through K. Ryerson, Cassandra Press, Boulder, CO.

Gurudas (1986) *Gem Elixirs and Vibrational Healing 2,* channeled through K. Ryerson, Cassandra Press, Boulder, CO.

Harold, E. (1987) *Crystal Healing,* Aquarian, Wellingborough.

Oldfield, H. (1988) *The Dark Side of the Brain. New Discoveries in Kirlian Photography and Crystal Energies,* Element Books, Longmead.

Raphaell, K. (1985) *Crystal Enlightenment,* Aurora, New York.

Raphaell, K. (1987) *Crystal Healing,* Aurora, New York.

Walker, D. (DaEL) (1983) *The Crystal Book,* Crystal Company, Sunol, CA.

Organizations

ASSOCIATION OF CRYSTAL HEALING THERAPISTS, 5 Sunnymede Vale, Holcombe Brook, Bury, Lancs BL0 9RR

CRYSTAL ACADEMY OF ADVANCED HEALING ARTS, PO Box 3208, Taos, New Mexico 87571

CRYSTAL RESEARCH FOUNDATION, 37 Bromley Road, St Anne's on the Sea, Lancashire FY8 1PQ Tel: (0253) 723735

SCHOOL OF ELECTRO-CRYSTAL THERAPY, 117 Long Drive, South Ruislip HA4 0HL

7

Specialized sources: dance therapy to psychosynthesis

DANCE THERAPY

This type of therapy involves the use of all kinds of dance and its therapeutic, meditative and magical qualities to help people grow. Dance therapy is used in a variety of settings: from the health service to the social services.

Resources

REFERENCE ITEMS

The Creative Tree. Edited by Gina Levete (Wilton, Salisbury: Michael Russell, 1987).
This book includes a section on dance and dance therapy training courses.

PERIODICALS

American Dance Therapy Association Newsletter (Columbia, MD: American Dance Therapy Association, 1967–).
This publication contains news of the ADTA, its activities and members.

American Journal of Dance Therapy. Edited by Rachael Harris (Columbia, MD: American Dance Therapy Association). Twice a year.

This professional journal contains refereed articles and book reviews.

Dance Theatre Journal (London: Laban Centre, 1983–). Quarterly.
New Dance (Bradford: New Dance Publications, 1983–).

BOOKS

Anderson, W. (Ed) (1977) *Therapy and the Arts: Tools of Consciousness,* Harper & Row, New York.
Bernstein, P. (1979) *Eight Theoretical Approaches in Dance Movement Therapy,* Kendall & Hunt, Dubuque, IO.
Costonis, M. N. (Ed) (1978) *Therapy in Motion,* University of Illinois Press, Urbana, IL.
Espenak, L. (1981) *Dance Therapy: Theory and Applications,* Thomas, Springfield, IL.
Harris, C. (Ed) (1975) *Marian Chase: Her Papers,* ADTA, Columba, Maryland.
Harris, J. G. (1984) *A Practicum for Dance Therapy,* ADMT Publications, London.
Hartley, L. (1984) *Body-Mind Centering: A Therapeutic Approach to the Body and Movement,* ADMT Publications, London.
Jennings, S. (Ed) (1983) *Creative Therapy,* Kemble, London.
Lamb, W. and Watson, E. (1979) *Body Code: The Meaning in Movement,* Routledge & Kegan Paul, London.
Spence, P. (Ed) (1985) *Society and the Dance,* CUP, Cambridge.
West Payne, H. (1983) *An Introduction to Dance Movement Therapy,* ADMT Publications, London.

Organizations

AMERICAN DANCE THERAPY ASSOCIATION, 2000 Century Plaza, Columbia MD 21044

ASSOCIATION FOR DANCE MOVEMENT THERAPY (ADMT), 99 South Hill Park, London NW3 2SP

LABAN CENTRE FOR MOVEMENT AND DANCE, Goldsmith's College, University of London, London SE14 6NW

SESAME (MOVEMENT AND DRAMA IN THERAPY), Christ-church, 27 Blackfriars Road, London SE1 8NY

DRAMA THERAPY

Drama therapy involves the use of drama (in its broadest sense – masks, mime, puppetry and other forms are included under the title, drama) as a therapeutic medium.

Resources

REFERENCE ITEMS

The Creative Tree. Edited by Gina Levete (Wilton, Salisbury: Michael Russell, 1987).
This book contains an international directory which includes sections on: drama/theatre; puppetry; drama therapy courses; and puppetry training courses.

PERIODICALS

Drama Therapy Bulletin (St Albans, Herts: Dramatherapy Consultants).
Journal of Dramatherapy (York: British Association of Dramatherapists).

BOOKS

Barker, C. (1977) *Theatre Games,* Methuen, London.
Bittleston, G. (1978) *The Healing Art of Glove Puppetry,* Floris Books, Edinburgh.
Bolton, G. (nda) *Towards a Theory of Drama in Education,* Longman, London.
Hodgson, J. (1977) *Uses of Drama: Acting as a Social and Educational Force,* Methuen, London.
Jennings, S. (1981) *Remedial Drama,* Black, London.
Jennings, S. (1986) *Creative Drama in Group Work,* Winslow Press, Winslow, Bucks.

Jennings, S. (Ed) (1986) *Dramatherapy: Theory and Practice for Teachers and Clinicians,* Croom Helm, London.
Langley, D. M. (1983) *Drama Therapy and Psychiatry,* Croom Helm, London.
Schattner, G. and Courtney, R. (1981) *Drama in Therapy* (Vol. 1), *Children* (Vol. 2), *Adults,* Drama Books, New York.
Scher, A. (1975) *100+ Ideas for Drama,* Heinemann, London.
Way, B. (1967) *Development Through Drama,* Longman, London.
Wethered, A. (1973) *Drama and Movement in Therapy,* M & E, London.

Organizations

BRITISH ASSOCIATION FOR DRAMATHERAPISTS, PO Box 98, Kirby Moorside, York YO6 6EX

KATHARINA SOMMER, The German Association for Therapeutic Puppetry, Parcusstrasse 13, 6100 Dramstadt, West Germany

MARIONETTE ET THERAPIE, 14 rue Saint-Benoit, 75006 Paris

DREAM THERAPY

Dreams have been used by people in many cultures as a means of coming to terms with the present and possibly the future. The Senoi are known for their dreams and methods of processing them. Freud published his leading work on dreams in 1900 and Jung extended and broadened this work. Since the early 1970s, dream therapy has grown and become a common therapy technique. Perls applied the techniques of gestalt therapy to dream work and his methods are widely used.

Resources

REFERENCE ITEMS

Welcome to the Magic Theatre, By Dick McLeester (Amherst, MA: Food for Thought, 1977).

Despite its age, this book is still a useful resource as it contains an annotated dream bibliography which includes many Jungian and gestalt references. There is also a USA dream directory.

PERIODICALS

Coat of Many Colours. Edited by Jeremy Taylor (San Rafael, CA: Dream Network Bulletin). Irregular.
This magazine contains articles on dreams, dream research and dreams and creativity. It also contains information about dream-work groups.

Dream International Quarterly. Edited by Les and Charles Jones (Hiroshima, 1982–). Quarterly.
This quarterly journal has an average of sixty A5 pages, is photocopied and has a print run of 200 copies. It is available from the editors at 1-17-7 Ushita Waseda, Higashi-Ku, Hiroshima 732, Japan. It includes fiction (prose and poetry) and non-fiction articles – all on the theme of dreaming.

Dream Network Bulletin. Edited by Chris Hudson (Charlottesville, VA: Dreamwork Network Bulletin). Bi-monthly.
This is a scholarly journal which deals with dreams from an anthropological and psychological perspective. It contains a forum for the exchange of readers' experiences and research and it also provides a listing of dreamwork conferences, workshops and conferences in the USA.

Dreamworks. Edited by Marsha Kinder (New York: Human Sciences Press). Quarterly.
This interdisciplinary journal covers the dream process in relationship to arts and sciences.

Lucidity Letter (Cedar Falls, IA: University of Northern Iowa Dept of Psychology). Biannual.
This journal publishes reports on: research findings; observations; personal experiences; lucid dreaming; and related phenomena such as out-of-body experiences.

Sundance: The Community Dream Journal. Edited by Henry Reed (Virginia Beach, VA: Sundance Community Newsletter). Irregular.

This newsletter relates to the dreamwork methods and their practice as described in the *Sundance Dream Journals*, a set of books providing information and techniques on dreamwork – available from the author Henry Reed (503 Lake Dr., Virginia Beach, VA 23451).

BOOKS

Caligor, L. and May, R. (1968) *Dreams and Symbols,* Basic, New York.

Crisp, T. (1984) *The Instant Dream Book,* Spearman, London.

Faraday, A. (1972) *Dream Power,* Berkley Publishing, E Rutherford, NJ.

Faraday, A. (1974) *The Dream Game,* Harper & Row, Scranton, PA.
A useful book for anyone who wants to start exploring their dreams.

Freud, S. (1976) *The Interpretation of Dreams,* Penguin, Harmondsworth.

Garfield, P. (1976) *Creative Dreaming*, Futura, London.

Green, C. (1968) *Lucid Dreams,* Institute of Psychophysical Research, London.

Holzer, H. (1976) *The Psychic Side of Dreams,* Doubleday, New York.

Jenks, K. (1977) *Journey of a Dream Animal,* Pocket Books, New York.

Jung, C. G. (1969) *Man and his Dreams,* Doubleday, New York. (Aldus, London: 1984).
Useful introduction to dreams and symbols with a good bibliography.

Jung, C. G. (1974) *Dreams,* University Press, Princetown.
A classic book on the subject.

Mallon, B. (1987) *Women Dreaming,* Fontana, Douglas, Isle of Man.
A readable book, well indexed with a useful bibliography.

Shohet, R. (1985) *Dream Sharing,* Turnstone, Wellingborough.

Williams, S. K. (1982) *The Jungian–Senoi Dreamwork Manual,* Journey Press, USA.

FELDENKRAIS TECHNIQUE

The Feldenkrais techniques are methods of functional integration and awareness through movement.

Resources

REFERENCE ITEMS

The Feldenkrais Guild Directory. Edited by W. Williams (San Francisco: Feldenkrais Guild, 1984).
This is an international listing of members of the Feldenkrais Guild. It is a free publication.

BOOKS

Feldenkrais, M. (1972) *Awareness Through Movement: Health Exercises for Personal Growth,* Harper & Row, New York.
A key book on the Feldenkrais method.

Organizations

FELDENKRAIS GUILD, PO Box 11145, San Fransisco, CA 94101 Tel: (415) 550-8708

GESTALT THERAPY

Gestalt therapy was developed by Perls who created a form of therapy in which the client is encouraged to increase his or her level of awareness and sensitivity. Perhaps as a therapy it is best known for being that in which someone 'talks to a cushion' but it is actually much more than that: it is a whole range of techniques which encourage the clients to increase their awareness and integrate their separate parts as 'many parts make the whole'.

Publishers

SELF THERAPY PRESS, 340 Santa Monica Avenue, Menlo Park, CA 94025, USA

Resources

REFERENCE ITEMS

The Gestalt Directory. Edited by Joe Wysong (Highland, NY: Center for Gestalt Development, 1985).
A directory of gestalt practitioners and training establishments.

PERIODICALS

The Gestalt Journal. Edited by Joe Wysong (Highland, NY: Center for Gestalt Development). Biannual.
This journal includes articles, book reviews and notes on activities of the Center.

Psychotherapy Newsletter. Edited by Joe Wysong (Highland, NY: Center for Gestalt Development). Quarterly.
This journal includes articles, news items, and book and periodical reviews.

BOOKS

Downing, J. (Ed) (1976) *Gestalt Awareness: Papers from the San Francisco Gestalt Institute,* Harper & Row, New York; London.
Dye, A. and Hackney, H. (1975) *Gestalt Approaches in Counseling,* Houghton Mifflin, Boston.
Fagan, J. and Shepherd, I. L. (Eds) (1972) *Gestalt Therapy Now,* Penguin, Harmondsworth.
A collection of essays which include theory and case histories. There is also an interview with Laura Perls.
Hatcher, C. and Himelstein, P. (Eds) (1976) *The Handbook of Gestalt Therapy,* Aronson, New York.
This book contains a series of articles.

144

Houston, G. (1982) *The Red Book of Gestalt,* Rochester Foundation, London.
A practical and concise book on gestalt therapy with many line drawings. This book provides a very good introduction to this subject.
Latner, J. (1974) *The Gestalt Therapy Book,* Bantam, New York.
Passons, W. R. (1975) *Gestalt Approaches in Counseling,* Holt, Rinehart & Winston, New York.
Perls, F. S. (1951) *Gestalt Therapy: Excitement and Growth in the Human Personality,* Julian Press, New York. (Souvenir, London, 1972).
Perls, F.S. (1971) *Gestalt Therapy Verbatim,* Bantam, New York.
One of the definitive books on this subject.
Perls, F. S. (1976) *The Gestalt Approach,* Bantam, New York.
Schiffman, M. (1971) *Gestalt Self Therapy,* Self Therapy Press, Menlo Park, CA.
A practical book which describes how to start doing self-help therapy at home, alone.
Stevens, J. O. (1973) *Awareness: Exploring Experimenting Experiencing,* Bantam, New York.
This useful book contains dozens of gestalt-based exercises.
Stevens, J. O. (Ed) (1975) *Gestalt Is,* Real People Press, Moab.
A collection of papers including a number by Perls.

Organizations

THE OPEN CENTRE, 188 Old Street, London EC1 Tel: 01-549 9583

HYPNOTHERAPY

Hypnotherapy is a technique which involves the therapist or hypnotherapist inducing an altered state of consciousness in the client. While the client is in this state, he or she can be led on guided meditations, regressed into earlier or past life experiences, or listen to relaxation music.

See also 'Neurolinguistic programming' later in this chapter.

Information services

BRUNTSFIELD CENTRE FOR HYPNOTHERAPY AND PSYCHOTHERAPY, 8 Granville Terrace, Edinburgh EH10 4PQ
Provides an information service for practitioners and will undertake individual literature searches. It produces a number of bibliographies:

Eating Disorders – Overeating, Obesity, Anorexia Nervosa, Bulima – 1975–1985
Hypnosis, Smoking and the Addictions – 1975–1985
Hypnosis and the Treatment of Phobias – 1975–1985
Pain Control – 1975–1985
Regressions and the Hidden Observer – 1975–1985

Resources

REFERENCE ITEMS

Bibliography of Modern Hypnotism. By M. Dessoir (Berlin: Dunckner, 1888).
A useful source for anyone interested in historical aspects of this subject.

Hypnotherapy: A Survey of the Literature. By Margaret Brenman *et al* (New York: International Universities Press, 1947).
This book covers the following topics: history of hypnosis; mesmerism; theory of hypnosis; and Erickson. It contains detailed bibliographies.

Mind-Body Therapies. A Select Bibliography of Books in English. By Robin Monro, Joanna E. Trevelyan and Ruth West (London: Mansell, 1987).
The section on hypnotherapy in this bibliography contains 370 entries.

PERIODICALS

AGH Journal. Edited by Reg Sheldrick (Omaha, NE: American Guild of Hypnotherapists).
This journal is free to members and is primarily concerned with hypnotherapy techniques.
Hypnosis Reports. Edited by Richard Hart (New York: Power Publishers). Monthly.
This journal is aimed at counsellors, therapists and social workers.
Hypnotherapy Today. Edited by William Brink (McLean, VA: AAPH). Quarterly.
The Register. The Journal of the National Register of Hypnotherapists and Psychotherapists (Nelson, Lancs: NRHP). Biannual.
This well-produced journal contains news, articles, abstracts of current journal articles and book reviews.

BOOKS

Ambrose, G. and Newbold, G. (1957) *Hypnosis in Health and Sickness,* Staple, St Albans.
Anderson-Evangelista, A. (1981) *Hypnosis: A Journey into the Mind,* Arco, New York.
Arons, H. (1984) *Hypnosis for Speeding up the Learning Process,* Borden, New York.
Arons, H. (1984) *New Master Course in Hypnosis,* Borden, New York.
Arons, H. (1984) *Seven Best Techniques for Deepening Hypnosis,* Borden, New York.
Barber, T. X., Spanos, N. P. and Chaves, J. F. (1986) *Hypnosis: Imagination and Human Potentialities,* Pergamon, New York and Oxford.
Bernheim, H. (1957) *Suggestive Therapeutics,* translated by C. A. Herter, Associated Book Publishers, London.
Bloch, G. J. (1980) *Mesmerism: A Translation of the Original Medical and Scientific Writings of F. A. Mesmer,* Kaufmann, Los Altos, CA.
Chester, R. J. (1982) *Hypnotism in East and West: Twenty Hypnotic Methods,* Octagon, New York.

Edmunds, S. (1982) *Psychic Power of Hypnosis*, Aquarian, Wellingborough.

Erickson, M. H. (1946) *Post-Hypnotic Behaviour,*in *Twentieth Century Psychology*, Philosophical Press, New York.

Erickson, M. H. (1980) *Hypnotherapy: An Exploratory Casebook*, 2nd edn, Irvington, New York (includes two audio cassettes).

Erickson, M. H. (1980) *Hypnotic Investigation of Psychodynamic Processes*, 2nd edn, E. L. Rossi (Ed) Irvington, New York.

Erickson, M. H. (1982) *Hypnotic Alteration of Sensory, Perceptual and Psychophysiological Processes*, Irvington, New York.

Erickson, M. H. (1982) *Innovative Hypnotherapy*, 2nd edn, E. L. Rossi, (Ed) Irvington, New York.

Erickson, M. H., Hershman, H. S. and Secter, I. I. (1961) *The Practical Application of Medical and Dental Hypnosis*, Julian, New York.

Erickson, H. and Rossi, E. L. (1981) *Experiencing Hypnosis: Therapeutic Approaches to Altered States*, Irvington, New York (includes two audio cassettes).

Erickson, M. H., Rossi, E. L. and Rossi, S. I. (1976) *Hypnotic Realities: The Induction of Clinical Hypnosis and Forms of Direct Suggestions*, Irvington, New York.

Follas, L. (1980) *Hypnosis and the Higher Self*, Regency, London.

Francuch, P. D. (1982) *Principles of Spiritual Hypnosis*, Spiritual Advisory Press, Santa Barbara, CA.

Francuch, P. D. (1983) *Intensive Spiritual Hypnotherapy*, Spiritual Advisory Press, Santa Barbara, CA.

French, N. (1984) *Successful Hypnotherapy*, Thorsons, Wellingborough.

Gallwey, W. T. (1974) *The Inner Game of Tennis*, Jonathan Cape, London.

Gilligan, S. G. (1986) *Therapeutic Trances: The Cooperation Principle in Ericksonian Hypnotherapy*, Brunner/Mazel, New York.

Goldberg, B. (1983) *Past Lives, Future Lives: Accounts of Regression and Progression Through Hypnosis*, Borgo, San Bernardino, CA.

Grinder, J., DeLozier, J. and Bandler, R. (1977) *Patterns of Hypnotic Techniques of Milton H. Erickson, MD. Vol. 2*, Meta Pubs, Culpertino, CA.

Haley, J. (1967) *Advanced Techniques of Hypnosis and Therapy: Selected Papers of Milton H. Erickson,* Grune, New York.

Hilgard, E. R. (1965) *Hypnotic Susceptibility,* Harcourt, Brace and World, New York.

Hilgard, E. R. (1968) *The Experience of Hypnosis. A Shorter Version of 'Hypnotic Susceptibility',* Harcourt, Brace and World, New York.

Hilgard, E. R. (1986) *Divided Consciousness: Multiple Controls in Human Thought and Action,* 2nd edn, Wiley, Chichester.

Kaplan, S. J. (1977) *Hypnotherapy Techniques and Tactics,* Rickard, New York.

Karle, H. W. A. (1988) *Hypnosis and Hypnotherapy: A Patient's Guide,* Thorsons, Wellingborough.

Karle, H. W. A. and Boys, J. (1987) *Hypnotherapy: A Practical Handbook,* Free Association, London.

Kuhn, L. and Russo, S. (1958) *Modern Hypnosis,* Wiltshire, North Hollywood, CA.

Lesser, D. (1985) *I Heard Every Word. Hypnotherapy Explained,* Curative Hypnotherapy Examination Committee, Birmingham.

Marcuse, F. L. (1964) *Hypnosis Throughout the World,* Charles C. Thomas, Springfield, IL.

Markham, U. (1987) *Hypnosis. Alternative Health,* Macdonald Optima, London.

Oakley, G. (1985) *Secrets of Self Hypnosis,* Thorsons, Wellingborough.

Ornstein, R. (1985) *Self-Hypnosis and Scientific Self-Suggestion,* Thorsons, Wellingborough.

Ousbey, W. J. (1984) *Theory and Practice of Hypnotism,* 2nd edn, Thorsons, Wellingborough.

Overholser, L. C. (1983) *Ericksonian Hypnosis: Principles of Theory and Practice,* Irvington, New York.

Rossi, E. L. (Ed) (1983) *Healing in Hypnosis: Seminars, Workshops and Lectures of Milton H. Erickson,* Irvington, New York (includes an audio cassette).

Shone, R. (1985) *Advanced Autohypnosis,* Thorsons, Wellingborough.

Shone, R. (1985) *Autohypnosis: A Step by Step Guide to Self-Hypnosis,* Thorsons, Wellingborough.

Shreeve, C. and Shreeve, D. (1984) *The Healing Power of*

Hypnotism: How It Is and How It Works, Thorsons, Wellingborough.
Sleet, R. (1983) *Hypnotherapy: A Patient's Guide,* Element Books, Salisbury.
Zilbergeld, B., Edelstein, M. G. and Araoz, D. L. (1986) *Hypnosis: Questions & Answers,* Norton, New York.

Organizations

AMERICAN ASSOCIATION OF PROFESSIONAL HYPNO-THERAPISTS, PO Box 731, McLean, VA 22101 Tel: (703) 448-9623

AMERICAN GUILD OF HYPNOTHERAPISTS, 7117 Fornam Street, Omaha, NE 68132 Tel: (402) 397-1502

ASSOCIATION OF HYPNOTISTS AND PSYCHOTHERAP-ISTS, 25 Market Square, Nelson, Lancs BB9 7LP UK Tel: (0282) 699378

MASSAGE

Massage work is a healing skill which can be used to facilitate body maintenance and relaxation. As well as being a therapy in its own right, it forms an important part of acupressure, aromotherapy, polarity therapy, Reichian therapy, reflexology, rolfing, and Shiatsu.

Resources

REFERENCE ITEMS

Massage and Bodywork Resource Guide of North America. Edited by Shane Watson (Leucadia, CA: Orenda/Unity Press, 1983).
This guide includes details of: massage schools; colleges; work-shops; seminars; professional associations; product listings. Its coverage is not restricted to North America. It also contains a good bibliography.

Massageworks: A Practical Encyclopedia of Massage Techniques. By Lawrence D. Baloti and Lewis Harrison (New York: GD/ Perigree Book/Putnam, 1983).
This is a clearly written book which contains excellent drawings, photographs and charts. The book includes: definitions of twenty-five massage, bodywork and manipulation systems; and addresses of massage centres and institutes in the USA.

PERIODICALS

The Massage Journal. Edited by Marilyn Frender (Kingsport, TN: American Massage Therapy Association). Quarterly.
This is the official Association journal and it contains news, conference reports and other items of interest to massage professionals.

The Massage Magazine. Edited by Robert Calvert (Kealakekua, HI: Massage Magazine). Bi-monthly.
This magazine aims to promote communication of ideas, techniques and awareness about massage, and other healing arts.

Stroking Times. Edited by David Linton (Springfield, PA: Stroking Community). Monthly.
This magazine provides a mine of useful information about training courses, workshops, equipment and support groups.

BOOKS

Downing, G. (1972) *The Massage Book,* Random House, New York.
Downing, G. (1974) *Massage and Meditation,* Random House, New York.
Gunther, B. (1973) *Massage,* Academy Editions, London.
Hoffer, J. (1977) *Total Massage,* Grossett & Dunlap, New York.
Miller, R. D. (1975) *Psychic Massage,* Harper & Row, New York.
Rush, A. K. (1974) *Getting Clear: Bodywork for Women,* Wildwood, Aldershot.
Tappon, F. M. (1978) *Healing Massage Techniques: A Study of Eastern and Western Methods,* Reston, Reston, VA.
Triance, E. R. (1984) *Massage at your Fingertips,* Science of Life, London.

Tulku, T. (1978) *Kum Nye Relaxation*. Part 1: *Theory, Preparation, Massage*. Part 2: *Movement Exercises,* Dharma, Berkeley, CA.
'Kum Nye relaxation is a gentle healing system which relieves stress, transforms negative patterns, helps us to be more balanced and healthy, and increases our enjoyment and appreciation of life.' Kum Nye includes energy, movement, massage and meditation exercises. It is an Eastern way originating in Tibet.
Young, C. (1975) *Massage: The Touching Way to Sensual Health,* Bantam, London.

Organizations

INDEPENDENT REGISTER OF MANIPULATIVE THERA-PISTS LTD, 106 Crowstone Rd, Westcliff-on-Sea, Essex SS0 8LQ Tel: (0702) 48820

INDEPENDENT THERAPISTS EXAMINING COUNCIL (ITEC), 3 The Planes, Bridge Road, Chertsey, Surrey Tel: (09328) 66839

LONDON SCHOOL OF MANIPULATIVE THERAPIES, 103 Prince Albert Square, Redhill, Surrey RH1 JAR

MUELLER COLLEGE, 4607 Park Boulevard, San Diego, CA 92116 Tel: (619) 291-9811

NORTHERN INSTITUTE OF MASSAGE/NORTHERN COLLEGE OF PHYSICAL THERAPIES, 100 Waterloo Road, Blackpool FY4 1AW Tel: (0235) 403548

WEST LONDON SCHOOL OF THERAPEUTIC MASSAGE, 69b Princes Square, London W2 Tel: 01-229 4250

MEDITATION

Meditation is a tool which can be used to help clear and relax the mind and body and obtain a sense of inner peace. There are many different forms of meditation: concentrative or absorptive meditation (examples include working with a word, a symbol, a movement, a picture or something else); expressive meditation such as a dynamic meditation which involves special breathing, movement and noise; a negative meditation where all forms and expressions are eliminated, such as some yoga meditations; and a facilitative way which opens awareness to what it is. Rowan describes this in more detail ('Meditation and therapy: a quadrant process,' in *Self and Society*, Vol.14, No.1, Jan/Feb 1986, pp. 2–5.).

Resources

REFERENCE ITEMS

Inner Development. By Cris Popenoe (Harmondsworth: Penguin, 1979).
Contains sections on meditation and transcendental meditation.

International Meditation Bibliography. 1950–1982. By Howard R. Jarrell (Metuchen, NJ: Scarecrow, 1985).
See entry under 'Bibliographies' in Chapter 5.

PERIODICALS

Articles on meditation practice may be found in many general journals on yoga or Buddhism, for example. They may also be found in journals such as *Journal of Transpersonal Psychology* and *Journal of Humanistic Psychology*.

Meditation. Edited by Patrick and Tricia Harbala (Van Nuys, CA: Intergroup for Planetary Oneness). Quarterly.
This journal serves to explore and promote meditation and also provide a source for meditational activities and organizations.

BOOKS

Ajaya, S. (Ed) (1977) *Meditational Therapy,* Himalayan International Institute of Yoga Science and Philosophy of the USA, Glenview, IL.
This book looks at the therapeutic use of meditation and Hatha Yoga.

Baker, M. E. P. (1973) *Meditation: A Step Beyond with Edgar Cayce,* Doubleday, Garden City, NY.

Chaitow, L. (1983) *Relaxation and Meditation Techniques,* Thorsons, Wellingborough.

Coleman, D. (1977) *The Varieties of the Meditative Experience,* Rider, London.

Dass, R. (1974) *The Only Dance There Is,* Anchor, Garden City, NY.

Dass, R. (1978) *Journey of Awakening: A Meditator's Guidebook,* Bantam, New York.

A readable book which provides a helpful introduction to meditation.

Hanh, T. N. (1976) *The Miracle of Mindfulness,* Beacon, Boston.

Herrigel, E. (1972) *Zen in the Art of Archery,* Routledge, London.

Humphrey, C. (1973) *Concentration and Meditation,* Watkins, London.

Joy, W. B. (1979) *Joy's Way,* Tarcher, Los Angeles.

Laurie, S. G. and Tucker, M. J. (1983) *Centering. A Guide to Inner Growth,* Destiny, New York.

A clearly written book which puts meditation in the context of spiritual and psychic development.

LeShan, L. (1977) *How to Meditate,* Wildwood, Aldershot.

Levine, S. (1979) *A Gradual Awakening,* Century, London.

A good introduction to general meditation techniques.

Naranjo, C. and Ornstein, R. E. (1976) *On the Psychology of Meditation,* Penguin, Harmondsworth.

Progoff, I. (1980) *The Practice of Process Meditation,* Dialogue House Library, New York.

Puryear, M. A. (1978) *Healing Through Meditation and Prayer,* ARE Press, Virginia Beach, VA.

Shastri, H. P. (1985) *Meditation Its Theory and Practice,* Shanti Sadan, London.

Trungpa. C. (1969) *Meditation in Action,* Shambhala, Boulder, CO.

Tulku, T. (1978) *Kum Nye Relaxation.* Part 1: *Theory, Preparation, Massage.* Part 2: *Movement Exercises,* Dharma, Berkeley, CA.

See under 'Massage'.

Welwood, J. (1983) *Awakening the Heart: East/West Approaches to Psychotherapy and the Healing Relationship,* Shambhala, Boulder, CO.

A series of essays and commentaries some of which explore meditation. Brief bibliography.
Whitman, A. (1976) *Meditation: Journey to the Self,* Simon and Schuster, New York.

METAMORPHIC TECHNIQUE, REFLEXOLOGY, ZONE THERAPY

These are all healing skills which work at the level of the foot although their effects may be on the psychological level too. They are based on the theory that there are areas or reflex points on the feet and hands that correspond to each organ, gland and structure in the body. By working on these points the therapist can reduce physical and emotional problems.

Resources

REFERENCE ITEMS

Mind-Body Therapies. A Select Bibliography of Books in English. Compiled by Robin Monro, Joanna E. Trevelyan and Ruth West (London: Mansell, 1987).
This book has a section on the foot therapies.

BOOKS

Bayley, D. E. (1984) *Reflexology Today,* Thorsons, Wellingborough.
Bendix, G. J. (1976) *Pressure Point Therapy,* Thorsons, Wellingborough.
Bergson, A. and Tuchak, V. (1974) *Zone Therapy,* Pinnacle, New York.
Bergson, D. (1977) *The Foot Book: Healing the Body Through Reflexology,* Barnes & Noble, New York.
Goosman-Legger, A. (1986) *Zone Therapy Using Foot Massage,* translated by T. Langham and P. Peters, Daniel, Saffron Walden.
Kaye, A. and Matchan, D. C. (1979) *Reflexology: Techniques of Foot Massage for Health and Fitness,* Thorsons, Wellingborough.

Kunz, K. and Kunz, B. (1984) *The Complete Guide to Reflexology*, Thorsons, Wellingborough.

Marquardt, H. (1983) *Reflex Zone Therapy of the Feet: A Textbook of Therapy*, Thorsons, Wellingborough.

Saint-Pierre, G. and Boater, D. (1984) *The Metamorphic Technique: The Principles and Practice*, Element Books, Salisbury, Wilts.

Saint-Pierre, G. and Thompson, B. D. (1981) *Principles and Practice of the Metamorphic Technique*, Metamorphic Association, London.

Sega, M. (1979) *Reflexology*, Whitmore, Ardmore, PA.

Wagner, F., with Schwarz, H. (1987) *Reflex Zone Massage: Handbook of Therapy and Self-Help*, Thorsons, Wellingborough.

Organizations

BRITISH REFLEXOLOGY ASSOCIATION, 12 Pond Road, London SE3 5RB Tel: 01-852 6062

INTERNATIONAL INSTITUTE OF REFLEXOLOGY, PO Box 34, Harlow, Essex CM17 0LT

METAMORPHIC ASSOCIATION, 67 Ritherdon Road, London SW17 8QE

MUSIC THERAPY

Music therapy is one of the oldest forms of therapy and there is evidence of its use in past Greek and Egyptian civilizations. Music's properties as a medium for self-expression, self-knowledge, communication and creativity are used by music therapists in many different ways. Clients may be encouraged to create or respond to music. The meditative and relaxation aspects of music may be incorporated into the therapeutic process. Chants and mantras may be intoned to help a person explore and develop his or her consciousness.

Resources

REFERENCE ITEMS

The Creative Tree. Edited by Gina Levete (Wilton, Salisbury: Michael Russell, 1987).
This book has an international directory which contains the following sections: music; music therapy training courses; organizations for information on music therapy training.

Music Periodical Literature: An Annotated Bibliography of Indexes and Bibliographies. By Joan M. Meggett (Metuchen, NJ: Scarecrow, 1978).
Music Therapy Sources Book. By C. Schulberg (New York: Human Sciences, 1981).

PERIODICALS

British Journal of Music Therapy (London: BSMT). Three times a year.
This journal is a tool for keeping BSMT members up to date. It contains articles, news and book reviews.

ICM West Newsletter. Edited by Helen Bonny (Port Townsend, WA: ICM). Three times a year.
This journal is concerned with music and personal growth.

Journal of Music Therapy (Washington, DC: NAMT).

The Rose Window. Edited by Kay Gardner (Stoningon, ME: Healing Through Arts). Irregular.
This newsletter contains well-writen articles and news items.

BOOKS

Alvin, J. (1983) *Music Therapy,* Clare, London.
Armstrong, F. (1987) *'The Voice is the Muscle of the Soul',* in L. Saunders (Ed) *Glancing Fires: An Investigation into Women's Creativity,* The Women's Press, London.
Clynes, M. (Ed) (1982) *Music Mind and Brain,* Plenum, New York.

Crandall, J. (1986) *Self-Transformation Through Music,* Theosophical, Wheaton, IL.

Drury, N. (1986) *Music for Inner Space – Techniques,* Prism, London.

Gaston, E. (1968) *Music in Therapy,* Macmillan, London.

Halpern, S. (1985) *Sound Health,* Harper and Row, San Francisco.

Hamel, P. M. (1978) *Through Music to the Self,* Compton, Salisbury.

Heline, C. (1943) *Healing and Regeneration Through Music,* Rowny Press, Santa Barbara, CA, 1970.

McLaughlin, T. (1970) *Music and Communication,* Faber, London.

Pratt, R. R. (Ed) (c1987) *Rehabilitation and Human Well-Being: The Fourth International Symposium on Music: August 1–5, 1985, New York City,* University Press of America, Lanham.

Priestley, M. (1975) *Music Therapy in Action,* Constable, London.

Rubinstein, M. (1986) *Music to My Ear,* Quartet, London.

Rudd, E. (1980) *Music Therapy and its Relationship to Current Treatment Theories,* Magnamusic-Baton, St Louis, Miss.

Rudhyar, D. (1986) *The Magic of Tone and the Art of Music,* Dent, London.

Seashore, C. (1967) *Psychology of Music,* Dover, New York.

Watson, A. and Drury, N. (1987) *Healing Music,* Prism, Bridport, Dorset.

Organizations

AMERICAN ASSOCIATION FOR MUSIC THERAPY, 66 Morris Avenue, PO Box 359, Springfield NJ 07081

ASSOCIATION OF PROFESSIONAL MUSIC THERAPISTS, Steve Dunachie (Secretary), St Lawrence's Hospital, Caterham, Surrey

BRITISH SOCIETY FOR MUSIC THERAPY, Guildhall School of Music and Drama, Barbican, London EC2Y 8DT

INSTITUTE FOR CONSCIOUSNESS AND MUSIC, PO Box 173, Port Townsend, WA 98368 Tel: (206) 385-6160

NATIONAL ASSOCIATION OF MUSIC THERAPISTS, Suite 1000, 1133 Fifteenth Street NW, Washington DC 2005

NEUROLINGUISTIC PROGRAMMING

Neurolinguistic programming is a technique which has applications beyond the field of therapy to education, business and government. It was developed in the 1970s by Bandler and Grinder and offers a model of human experience and communication which can be used by therapists and others. Neurolinguistic programming has its roots in the work of famous therapists such as Perls and Satir and also in linguistics and computer science.

Bookshops

CHANGES BOOKSHOP (see Chapter 5) in London keeps practically all the books available on NLP in stock and publishes a special catalogue on this subject.

Resources

REFERENCE ITEMS

A directory of certified NLP practitioners is maintained by Not Ltd DOTAR (517 Mission Street, Santa Cruz, CA 95060).

BOOKS

Bandler, R. (1984) *Magic in Action,* Meta Publications, Cupertino, CA.
Includes many case studies.
Bandler, R. and Grinder, J. (1975) *The Structure of Magic,* Science & Behaviour Books, Paolo Alto, CA.
This book presents the Meta Model which is based on the principles of transformational grammar.
Bandler, R. and Grinder, J. (1975) *The Structure of Magic 2,* Science & Behaviour Books, Paolo Alto, CA.
This book follows on from Volume 1 and presents representational

systems and includes chapters on incongruity, fuzzy functions and family therapy.

Bandler, R. and Grinder, J. (1975) *Trance-Formations,* Science & Behaviour Books, Paolo Alto, CA.
Edited transcripts of workshops.

Bandler, R. and Grinder, J. (1979) *Frogs into Princes,* Real People's Press, Moab, Utah.
A classic book on this subject. It contains transcripts of workshops.

Bandler, R. and Grinder, J. (1979) *Reframing,* Real People's Press, Moab, Utah.
Another book which presents detailed aspects of NLP by presenting edited transcripts of workshops.

Bandler, R., Grinder, J. and Satir, V. (1976) *Changing with Families,* Science & Behaviour Books, Paolo Alto, CA.

Boas, P., with Brooks, J. (1984) *Advanced Techniques. Book 1. An NLP workbook,* Metamorphosis, Lake Oswago, OR.
This book includes many NLP exercises.

Cameron-Bandler, L. (1985) *Solutions,* FuturePace, San Rafael, CA.
A good introduction to the subject which covers the basic theories behind NLP. Specific examples relate to sex and relationship problems.

Cameron-Bandler, L., Gorden, D. and Lebeau, M. (1985) *The Emprint Method: A Guide to Reproducing Competence,* Future-Pace, San Rafael, CA.

Lewis, B. A. and Pucelik, F. (1982) *Magic Demystified: An Introduction to NLP,* Metamorphosis, Lake Oswago, OR.

Organizations

NLP TRAINING PROGRAM, 22 Upper Tooting Park, London SW17 7SR

NOT LTD DOTAR, 517 Mission Street, Santa Cruz, CA 95060

UK TRAINING CENTRE FOR NEURO-LINGUISTIC PROGRAMMING, 6 Ravenscourt Avenue, London NW11 ORY

UNLIMITED LTD, 1077 Smith Grade, Boony Doon, CA 95060

POLARITY THERAPY

Polarity therapy is a combination of Eastern and Western techniques which are aimed at freeing the body's energies and enabling them to flow. Polarity therapy was developed by Randolph Stone and involves cleansing diets, yogic exercises, manipulation and energy balancing.

Resources

BOOKS

Schiegl, H. (1987) *Healing Magnetism: The Transference of Vital Force Through Polarity Therapy,* Rider, London.
Siegal, A. (1987) *Polarity Therapy. The Power That Heals,* Prism, Bridport, Dorset.
This is a very readable and thorough introduction to this subject.
Stone, R. (1978) *Health Building,* Parameter Press, Orange County, CA.

Organizations

POLARITY THERAPY ASSOCIATION OF THE UK, 2 Leys Road, Cambridge Tel: (0223) 316364

PRIMAL THERAPY

Primal therapy allows the person in therapy to regress to what Arthur Janov (the founder of primal therapy) called the 'primal scene' and to reconnect with, own and discharge these feelings.

Resources

PERIODICALS

See 'The primal issue,' in *Self and Society,* Vol.5, No.6, June 1977.
See 'The primal issue revisited,' in *Self and Society,* Vol.15, No.2, March/April 1987.

See 'Voices from the past,' in *Self and Society,* Vol.15, No.4, July/August, 1987.

BOOKS

Albery, N. (1975) *How to Feel Reborn,* Regeneration Press, London.
Freundlich, D. (1975) 'Janov's Primal Theory of Neurosis and Therapy', in J. H. Masserman (Ed) *Current Psychiatric Therapies,* Grune and Stratton, New York.
Janov, A. (1971) *The Anatomy of Mental Illness,* Putnam, New York.
Janov, A. (1972) *The Primal Revolution,* Simon and Schuster, New York.
Janov, A. (1973) *The Feeling Child,* Simon and Schuster, New York.
Janov, A. (1973) *The Primal Scream* Doubleday, New York; Sphere, London.
Janov, A. (1988) *Primal Man,* Simon and Schuster, New York.
Rank, O. (nda) *The Trauma of Birth,* Torchbooks, New York.

PSYCHODRAMA

Psychodrama is a therapy developed by Moreno which works on the basis that acting out particular issues or situations with other people taking on roles (such as mother, father) in the given situation can be a therapeutic and healing process.

Resources

REFERENCE ITEMS

Bibliography of Psychodrama. Compiled by Valerie J. Greer and James M. Sacks (New York, 1973).

PERIODICALS

Federation of Trainers and Training Programs in Psychodrama Newsletter. Edited by Tom Schramski (Littleton, CA: FTTPP). Quarterly.

BOOKS

Blatner, H. A. (1973) *Acting In: Practical Applications of Psychodynamic Methods,* Springer, New York.
Ernst, S. and Goodison, L. (1981) *In Our Own Hands: A Book of Self-Help Therapy,* The Women's Press, London.
This book has a chapter which provides a very good summary of psychodrama.
Greenberg, I. A. (Ed) (1975) *Psychodrama: Theory and Therapy,* Souvenir, London.
Leveton, E. (1977) *Psychodrama: For the Timid Clinician,* foreword by V. Satir, Springer, New York.
Molony, V. (1971) *Psychodrama: A New Approach,* Impact, Dublin.
Moreno, J. (1953) *Who Shall Survive?,* Beacon, New York.
Moreno, J. (1975) *Psychodrama,* Beacon, New York.
Schutz, W. (1967) *Joy,* Penguin, Harmondsworth.
Starr, A. (1977) *Psychodrama: Rehearsal for Living,* Nelson-Hall, Chicago.
Yablonsky, L. (1976) *Psychodrama: Resolving Personal Problems Through Role Playing,* Basic, New York.

Organizations

FEDERATION OF TRAINERS AND TRAINING PROGRAMS IN PSYCHODRAMA, 6391 S Zenobia Court, Littleton, CO 80123

PSYCHOSYNTHESIS

Psychosynthesis was developed by Assagioli and is a process which helps to develop a healthy, whole person and enables the person to explore higher states of consciousness. Psychosynthesis uses a variety of techniques: affirmations; music therapy; symbolism; guided meditation; art; movement; gestalt; and imagery.

Resources

PERIODICALS

Institute of Psychosynthesis. Yearbook (London: Institute of Psychosynthesis, 1981-).
Synthesis (London: Psychosynthesis and Education Trust, 1977). Three volumes only.

BOOKS

Assagioli, R. (1965) *Psychosynthesis. A Manual of Principles and Techniques,* Turnstone, Wellingborough.
Brown, M. Y. (1983) *The Unfolding Self: Psychosynthesis and Counselling,* Psychosynthesis Press, New York.
Ferrucci, P. (1982) *What We May Be,* Turnstone, Wellingborough.
Hardy, J. (1987) *A Psychology with a Soul. Psychosynthesis in Evolutionary Context,* Routledge & Kegan Paul, London.
Weiser, J. and Yeomans, T. (Eds) (1985) *Readings in Psychosynthesis*, Institute for Studies in Education, Ontario.
Whitmore, D. (1986) *Psychosynthesis in Education. A Guide to the Joy of Learning,* Turnstone, Wellingborough.

PAMPHLETS

Assagioli wrote many articles and pamphlets which are available from the organizations listed below. Titles include:

The Balancing and Synthesizing of Opposites
Cheerfulness
Guidelines for Writing a Psychosynthesis Autobiography
The Inner Dialogue
Meditation
The Mystery of Self
The Resolution of Conflicts
The Seven Ways to Spiritual Realization

164

Training
Transpersonal Inspiration.

Organizations

CANADIAN INSTITUTE OF PSYCHOSYNTHESIS, 3496 Marlowe Avenue, Montreal, Quebec H4A 3L7

GREEK CENTRE FOR PSYCHOSYNTHESIS, Kyvelis 5, Athens 147

INSTITUTE OF PSYCHOSYNTHESIS, 1 Cambridge Gate, London NW1 4JN

ISTITUTO DI PSICOSINTESI, 16 via San Domenico, 50133 Florence

PSYCHOSYNTHESIS RESEARCH FOUNDATION, Room 1902, 40 East 49th Street, New York 10017

TRUST FOR THE FURTHERANCE OF PSYCHOSYNTHESIS & EDUCATION, 188-194 Old Street, London EC1V 9BP

8

Specialized sources: rebirthing to yoga

REBIRTHING

Rebirthing or conscious connected breathing is a powerful healing method . . . We use a simple breathing technique, with a new understanding of power of thought. We have found that by relaxing and releasing the breath, there is a corresponding dissolving of tensions in the body and the mind . . . Rebirthing involves a series of 'breathing sessions', usually weekly, which develop awareness, sensitivity and understanding of our self, our thoughts, and our emotions. There is a deepening sense of physical safety, of trust in relationships with other people, and of our own responsibility in life. The breathing we use is an easy, deep and connected breath in a rhythm which is natural and unique for each person.

(British Rebirth Society pamphlet)

Bookshops

A number of mail order services specialize in items (books and cassettes) on rebirthing.

THE CREATIVE SOURCE, PO Box 11024, Costa Mesa, CA 92627

HEAVEN ON EARTH BOOKS, 126 Elms Crescent, London SW4 8QR Tel: 01-673 0962

MANIFESTATIONS UNLIMITED, 96 Sandy Lane, Chorlton, Manchester M21 2TZ Tel: 061-861 0940

Resources

PERIODICALS

Breathe. Edited by Robert Moore (London: Breathe (C/o 18a Gt Percy Street, WC1X 9QP)). Quarterly.
This quarterly journal is a diary of events and news of interest to people involved in rebirthing in the UK. It includes a list of member rebirthers of the British Rebirth Society.

Breath Release (Beverly Hills: Breath release). Irregular.
This newsletter contains brief articles, workshop announcements and practitioners' advertisements.

Conscious Connection. Edited by Joe Moriaty (Sierraville, CA: Campbell Hot Springs). Monthly.
This is a newsletter of particular interest to people associated with the Campbell Hot Springs centre though its case studies may have a wider appeal.

The Immortal News (Philadelphia: Immortal News). Bi-monthly.
This newsletter contains articles and letters, as well as practitioner and workshop advertisments.

BOOKS

Albery, N. (1985) *How to Feel Reborn,* Regeneration Press, London.
Edmunds, K. (1980) *Rebirthing: A Transpersonal Growth System,* Synthesis International, San Diego, CA.
Laut, P. and Leonard, J. (1983) *Rebirthing: The Science of Enjoying All of Your Life,* Trinity Publications, Hollywood, CA.
Orr, L. and Ray, S. (1977) *Rebirthing in the New Age,* Celestial Arts, Berkeley.
Ray, S. (1983) *Celebration of Breath,* Celestial Arts, Berkeley.
Ray, S. (1987) *Loving Relationships,* Celestial Arts, Berkeley.

Organizations

BRITISH REBIRTH SOCIETY, Judith Collignon (Secretary), 22
Shirlock Road, London NW3 2HS Tel: 01-267 8739

REICHIAN THERAPY

Reichian therapy is based on Wilhelm Reich's ideas of the body's
tendencies to hold emotions in body armour and the aim of the
therapy is to dissolve the armour and so enable the energy to flow
freely.

Publishers

ORGONE INSTITUTE PRESS, New York

Resources

REFERENCE ITEMS

Bibliography on Orgone Biophysics. By James De Meo (Miami,
FL: James De Meo, 1985).
This bibliography covers the period from 1934 to 1984 and contains
about 400 references. It includes a list of all republished works by
Reich; a list of out-of-print materials; a list of works by Reich's co-
workers and others since his death; references to books, periodical
articles, unpublished papers and symposia reports. This bibliography does not include items focused on sex-economy, orgone
therapy, or the biopathies. It is available from the author (PO Box
161983, Miami, Florida 33116).

Wilhelm Reich. By David Boadella (London: Arkana, 1985).
This book contains a detailed bibliography which is divided into
the following sections: books by Wilhelm Reich; journals devoted
to bio-energetics and orgonomy; bibliographies; books about bioenergetics, orgonomy, Wilhelm Reich and allied subjects; addresses
of organizations.

PERIODICALS

A complete list (including periodicals which have ceased publication) can be obtained from *Wilhelm Reich: The Evolution of His Work* by David Boadella. Key English language periodicals include:

Energy and Character. Edited by David Boadella (Abbotsbury, Dorset: Abbotsbury Publications, 1970-). Three times a year. Contains academic articles, book reviews, announcements of forthcoming publications, details of workshops and events.

Journal of Biodynamic Psychology (details unavailable)
Journal of Orgonomy (New York: Orgonomic Publications, 1967–). Twice a year.
A collection of articles by Reichian practitioners.

BOOKS

Boadella, D. (1974) *Wilhelm Reich: The Evolution of His Work,* Regnery, Chicago.
An important review of Reich and his work. Useful bibliography.
Cattier, M. (1973) *The Life and Work of Wilhelm Reich,* Avon, New York.
Edmondson, E. and Totten, N. (in press) *Reichian Growth Work: Melting the Blocks to Life and Love,* Prism Press, Bridport, Devon.
Higgins, M. and Raphael, C. M. (Eds) (1972) *Reich Speaks of Freud,* Souvenir, London.
Mairowitz, D. Z. (1986) *Reich for Beginners,* Unwin, London.
Reich, W. (1949) *Character Analysis,* Farrar, New York.
One of the classic books on this subject.
Reich, W. (1961) *The Function of the Orgasm,* Farrar, New York.
A classic book on this subject.
Reich, W. (1974) *The Discovery of the Orgone. Volume 2. The Cancer Biopathy,* Vision Press, London.
Reich, W. (1975) *Early Writings,* Farrar, New York.
Reich, W. (1976) *People in Trouble,* Farrar, New York.
Reich, W. (1980) *Genitality in the Theory and Therapy of Neurosis,* Farrar, New York.

Organizations

A full list of organizations concerned with the work of Reich and Reichian therapy is given in *Wilhelm Reich: The Evolution of His Work*.

AMERICAN COLLEGE OF ORGONOMY, 515 East 88th Street, New York 10028

ENERGY STREAM (The Post Reichian Association), C/o 12 St Ann's Ave, Burley, Leeds LS4 2PJ

MOVIMENTO REICHIANO, Umberto Rostaing (Secretary), Via Medina 5, 80133 Naples, Italy

ORGONOMIC RESEARCH FOUNDATION, Box 104, Red Hill Road, Ottsville, Pennsylvania 18942

WILHELM REICH INSTITUTE FOR ORGONOMIC STUDIES, 84–87 Daniels Street, Jamaica, New York

REIKI

Reiki, or the radiance technique, is a therapy which has evolved as an amalgamation of Eastern and Western techniques. It involves the balancing and attuning of body energies.

Resources

PERIODICALS

Reiki Review (Madeira Beach, FL: American-International Reiki Association).
This newsletter contains news, short articles and letters.

BOOKS

Ray, B. (nda) *The Reiki Factor,* Radiance Associates, Florida.

Organizations

AMERICAN-INTERNATIONAL REIKI ASSOCIATION, PO Box 86038, St Petersburg, Florida 33783

ASSOCIATION OF REIKI THERAPISTS, 5 Delancey Passage, Delancey Street, Camden Town, London NW1 7NN Tel: 01-387 6761

ROLFING

Ida Rolf developed a method of massage which works on the connective tissues and corrects and rebalances posture.

Resources

BOOKS

Rolf, I. (1977) *Rolfing – the Integration of Human Structures,* Dennis Landmann, Santa Monica, CA.

Organizations

ROLFING ASSOCIATES, 61 Grantham Road, Chiswick, London W4 2RT

THE ROLF INSTITUTE, C/o 69 Marlborough Place, London NW8

SHAMANISM

Shamanism is a term coined by anthropologists to describe the processes and techniques used by tribal doctors/priests throughout

171

the world. They frequently use trance and consciousness-altering drugs and also techniques which are now labelled psychodrama, meditation and music therapy.

Shamanism is included in this book as the shaman literature contains a wealth of information relevant to modern therapists.

Libraries

STATE HISTORICAL SOCIETY, Madison, Wisconsin
The library here houses an enormous collection of native American periodicals.

Resources

REFERENCE ITEMS

American Indian Community Service Directory. Edited by Beatrice Chevalier (Chicago, IL: Native American Educational Services, 1984).
This directory represents more than 100 tribal groups in the Chicago area. It provides detailed information on contacts, services, businesses and publications (including newspapers).

Native American Directory. Edited by Fred Snyder (San Carlos, AZ: Native American Co-operative, 1982).
This directory covers Canada and the USA and includes information about reservations; associations; museums; performers; events and other native-owned or directed activities.

Native American Periodicals and Newspapers 1828–1982. Edited by James Danky (Westport, CT: Greenwood, 1984).
A definitive bibliography which includes more than 1100 titles.

Whole Again Resource Guide, 1986/87. By Tim Ryan and Patricia Case (Santa Barbara, CA: SourceNet, 1986).
Has a section called Native peoples.

PERIODICALS

Articles can be found in academic journals such as:

Acta Etnographica
American Anthropologist
Ethnology
Journal of American Folklore
Journal of Californian Anthropology

and also in special issues of journals such as:

'Shamanism and other approaches to the transpersonal,' in *Self and Society,* Vol.14, No.1, January/February 1986.

and in journals such as:

Shaman's Drum, Edited by Debra Carroll (Berkeley: Cross-Cultural Shamanism Network). Four issues a year.
This is a journal of experimental shamanism which includes articles, descriptions of personal experiences, resource lists, book reviews, a calendar of events and advertisements.

BOOKS

Achterberg, J. (1985) *Imagery in Healing: Shamanism and Modern Medicine,* Shambhala, Boston.
Andrews, L. (1984) *Flight of the Seventh Moon,* Harper & Row, San Francisco.
Andrews, L. (1984) *Medicine Woman,* Harper & Row, San Francisco.
Andrews, L. (1985) *Jaguar Woman,* Harper & Row, San Francisco.
Brownman, A. and Schwartz, S. (1979) *Spirits, Shamans and Stars,* Nouton, New York.
Castaneda, C. (1968) *The Teachings of Don Juan: A Yaqui Way of Knowledge,* University of California Press, Berkeley.
Castaneda, C. (1971) *A Separate Reality,* Simon and Schuster, New York.
Castaneda, C. (1972) *Journey to Ixtlan,* Simon and Schuster, New York.
Castaneda, C. (1974) *Tales of Power,* Simon and Schuster, New York.

Edsman, C. (1967) *Studies in Shamanism,* Almquist & Wiksalls, Boltackeri, AB.

Eliade, M. (1964) *Shamanism – Archaic Techniques of Ecstasy,* Princetown University Press, Princetown.

Halifax, J. (1975) *Shamanic Voices,* Dutton, New York; Penguin, Harmondsworth, 1979.

Halifax, J. (1982) *Shaman: Wounded Healer,* Crossroad, New York.

Harner, M. (1980) *Way of the Shaman: A Guide to Power and Healing,* Harper & Row, San Francisco.
This book has a valuable bibliography.

Jamal, M. (1987) *Shape Shifters: Shaman Women in Contemporary Society,* Arkana, New York.
This book contains: an introduction; profiles of fourteen present-day shaman women; a profile of a shamanic community. There is a brief bibliography.

Kakar, S. (1982) *Shamans, Mystics and Doctors,* Unwin, London.

Larson, S. (1976) *The Shaman's Doorway,* Harper & Row, London.

Osumi, I. and Ritchie, M. (1987) *The Shamanic Healer: The Healing World of Ikuko Osumi and the Traditional Art of Seiki-Jutsu,* Century, London.

Rogers, S. (1982) *Shaman: His Power and His Healing Power,* C. Thomas, Springfield, IL.

Organizations

CROSS-CULTURAL SHAMANISM NETWORK, PO Box 2636, Berkeley, CA 94702

SHIATSU MASSAGE

Shiatsu was developed in this century and in some ways appears to be similar to acupressure. It involves the application of pressure to particular points on the body and so helps blocked energy to be mobilized.

Resources

REFERENCE ITEMS

Mind-Body Therapies. A Select Bibliography of Books in English. By Robin Monro, Joanna E. Trevelyan and Ruth West (London: Mansell, 1987).
This bibliography has a detailed section on books on Shiatsu.

PERIODICALS

Shiatsu Society News (Kilbarchan, Renfrewshire: Shiatsu Society). Quarterly.
This magazine contains news, conference reports, articles and advertisements. It provides a good introduction to what is happening regarding Shiatsu in the UK.

BOOKS

Bergson, A. and Tuchak, V. (1980) *Shiatsu: Japanese Pressure Point Therapy,* Pinnacle Books, New York.
Blate, M. (1985) *Physical Fitness: Use of Shiatzu,* Arkana, London.
Namikoshi, T. (1972) *Shiatzu: Japanese Finger-Pressure Therapy,* Japan Publications, San Francisco.
Namikoshi, T. (1977) *Shiatzu Therapy. Theory and Practice,* Wehmann Bros, New Jersey.
Namikoshi, T. (1981) *The Complete Book of Shiatsu Therapy,* Japan Publications, Tokyo.
Namikoshi, T. (1985) *Shiatsu + Stretching,* Japan Publications, Tokyo.
Ohashi, W. (1978) *Do-it-Yourself Shiatsu: How to Perform the Ancient Japanese Art of Acupuncture Without Needles,* Unwin, London.
Schultz, W. (1983) *Shiatsu: Japanese Finger Pressure Therapy,* Blandford, Poole, Dorset.
Yamamoto, S. (1979) *Barefoot Shiatsu,* Japan Publications, Tokyo.

Organizations

SHIATSU SOCIETY, 19 Langside Park, Kilbarchan,Renfrewshire
PA10 2EP

SPIRITUAL HEALING

Spiritual healing is a term used to describe non-physical healing
and includes absent healing and contact healing. Spiritual healing
may involve working with a person's energy field and chakras or
working with non-physical entities.

There is a vast literature on this subject and the items cited below
represent a selection.

Resources

BOOKS

Bailey, A. E. (1953) *Esoteric Healing*, Lucis, New York and
London.
Beasley, V. (1979) *Subtle-Body Healing*, University of the Trees
Press, Boulder Creek, CA.
Bek, L. and Pullar, P. (1986) *The Seven Levels of Healing*, Rider,
London.
Gordon, R. (1978) *Your Healing Hands*, Unity Press, California.
Hammond, S. (1983) *We Are All Healers*, Turnstone,
Wellingborough.
Harold, E. (1980) *Healing for the Aquarian Age*, Spiritual
Venturers Association, Ilfracombe, Devon.
Harvey, D. (1983) *The Power to Heal*, Aquarian, Wellingborough.
Kripper, S. and Villoldo, A. (1987) *The Realms of Healing*, 3rd
edn, Celestial Arts, Berkeley, CA.
Lansdowne, Z. F. (1986) *The Chakras and Esoteric Healing*,
Weiser, York Beach, MA.
Locker, L. (1985) *Healing All and Everything*, Element Books,
Shaftesbury, Dorset.
MacManaway, B., with Turcan, J. (1983) *Healing*, Thorsons,
Wellingborough.

176

Meek, G. W. (Ed) (1977) *Healers and the Healing Process,* Theosophical Publishing House, Wheaton, IL.
Sherwood, K. (1985) *The Art of Spiritual Healing,* Llewellyn New Times, St Paul, MN.
Wallace, A. and Henkin, B. (1981) *The Psychic Healing Book,* Turnstone, Wellingborough.

Organizations

CHURCHES COUNCIL FOR HEALTH AND HEALING, Marylebone Road, London NW1 5LT

NATIONAL FEDERATION OF SPIRITUAL HEALERS, Old Manor Farm Studio, Church Street, Sunbury-on-Thames, Middlesex TW16 6RG

T'AI CHI

T'ai chi is the Taoist practice of bringing the energy into harmony between the body and its environment. It is a form of moving meditation, self-defence and preventive health care. It involves subtle body movements through formalized exercises.

BOOKS

Chen, Y. K. (1971) *T'ai Chi Ch'uan: Its Effects and Practical Applications,* Unicorn Press, Hong Kong.
Chung-liang Huang, A. (1973) *Embrace Tiger, Return to Mountain – the Essence of T'ai chi,* Real People's Press, Moab, Utah,
Delza, S. (1961) *T'ai Chi Chuan,* Cornerstone Library, New York.
Horwitz, T., and Kimmelman, S., with Lui, H. H. (1982) *T'ai Chi Ch'uan. The Technique of Power,* Rider, London.
Huang, W. (1973) *Fundamentals of T'ai Chi Ch'uan,* South Sky Book Co, Hong Kong.
Liang, T. T. (1974) *T'ai Chi Ch'uan for Health and Self-Defense,* Redwing, Boston.
Maisel, E. (1963) *T'ai Chi for Health,* Dell, New York.

Man-ch'ing, C. (1962) *T'ai Chi Chuan: A Simplified Method of Calisthenics,* Shih Chung T'ai chi Chuan Center, Taiwan.
Man-ch'ing, C. and Smith, R. (1967) *T'ai Chi: The 'Supreme Ultimate' Exercise for Health, Sport and Self-Defense,* Charles Tuttle, Rutland, VE.
Ying-arng, L. (1968) *Lee's Modified Tai Chi for Health,* Unicorn Press, Hong Kong.

TRADITIONAL HEALING

Traditional healers are found in all cultures and heal dis-ease states at many different levels. Their involvement in the healing of physical dis-eases has meant that there is interest in this form of healing from the medical establishment, for example the World Health Organization, and consequently a body of medical literature on this topic.

The world of traditional healers overlaps with that of shamans and the reader is advised to also consult 'Shamanism,' above.

Resources

REFERENCE ITEMS

A useful introduction to the information sources on African traditional healers is the following article:

'African traditional medicine and health care programs: information sources and publishing opportunities'. By Stephen A. Osiobe, in *Alternative Medicine*, Vol.1, No.4, 1986, pp.329–339.

Traditional Medicine: Implications for Ethnomedicine, Ethnopharmacology, Maternal and Child Health, Mental Health, and Public Health: An Annotated Bibliography of Africa, Latin America, and the Caribbean. By Ira E. Harrison and Sheila Cosminsky (New York: Garland, 1976).

Traditional Medicine. Vol. 2. 1976-1981: An Annotated Bibliography of Africa, Latin America, and the Caribbean. By Sheila Cosminsky and Ira E. Harrison (New York: Garland, 1984).

178

Traditional medical bibliographies also contain items on traditional healing. Examples include:

Health Sciences Information Sources. By Ching-Chih Chen (Cambridge, MA: MIT, 1981).
Information Sources in the History of Medicine. Edited by Pieto Corsi and Paul Weindling (London: Butterworths, 1983).
Information Sources in the Medical Sciences. Edited by L. T. Morton and S. Godbolt (London: Butterworths, 1984).
Medical Information: A Profile. By Barry Strickland-Hodge and Barbara Allan (London: Mansell, 1986).

PERIODICALS

Articles can be found in the following academic periodicals:

Alternative Medicine
American Journal of Public Health
Journal of Tropical Medicine and Hygiene
Medical Anthropology
Social Science and Medicine
Tropical and Geographical Medicine
World Health Forum
WHO Chronicle

BOOKS

Bannerman, R. H., Burton, J. and Wen-Chieh, C. (Eds) (1983) *Traditional Medicine and Health Care Coverage,* WHO, Geneva.
Barbeau, M. (1958) *Medicine-Men on the North Pacific Coast,* National Museum of Canada Bulletin No.152. Anthropological Series No.42, Department of Northern Affairs and National Resources, Ottawa.
Djukanovic, V. D. and Mach, E. P. (Eds) (1975) *Alternative Approaches to Meeting Basic Health Needs in Developing Countries,* a joint UNICEF/WHO study. WHO, Geneva.
Jilek, W. G. (1974) *Salish Indian Mental Health and Cultural Changes: Psychohygienic and Therapeutic Aspects of the Guardian Spirit Ceremonial,* Holt Reinhart & Winston, Toronto and Montreal.

Meek, G. W. (Ed) (1977) *Healers and the Healing Process,* Theosophical Publishing House, Wheaton, IL.

Ngubane, H. (1977) *Body and Mind in Zulu Medicine,* Academic Press, New York.

WHO Regional Office for Africa, Brazzaville, (1970) *African Traditional Medicine: Report of an Expert Group,* AFRO Technical Report Series, No. 1.

YOGA

Yoga is a system of personal development which encompasses body, mind and spirit. It originated in India and involves movement, breathing and meditation techniques. Today, there are many schools of yoga each offering their own system.

Resources

REFERENCE ITEMS

Bibliography of Research Literature on Yoga. By Robin Monro, Danny Kalish and A. K. Ghosh (Cambridge, UK: Yoga Biomedical Trust, 1986).
This bibliography contains about 1500 references. It is held on a computerized database.

International Meditation Bibliography 1950–1982. By Howard Jarrell (Metuchen, NJ: Scarecrow, 1985).
This bibliography contains many entries on yoga as seen from the viewpoint of a meditative tool.

International Yoga Bibliography. By Howard Jarrell (Metuchen, NJ: Scarecrow, 1981).
This bibliography contains 1731 entries: books, journals and magazine articles. The entries are not annotated.

Mind-Body Therapies. A Select Bibliography of Books in English. By Robin Monro, Joanna E. Trevelyan, and Ruth West (London: Mansell, 1987).

The first section of this bibliography covers yoga and contains 515 references.

Whole Again Resource Guide, 1986/87. By Tim Ryan and Patricia J. Case (Santa Barbara, CA: SourceNet, 1986).
This edition contains a section on yoga which lists references to many periodicals.

Yoga Teachers Directories: Diploma Awards. Anon (Leicester: Barwell, 1982).

PERIODICALS

Specialized periodicals which are written by and, to a certain extent, for people following a particular path are not included here. They can be tracked down using *Whole Again Resource Guide* and *A Pilgrim's Guide to Planet Earth.* Today, many general magazines on yoga are available through commercial newsagents such as W H Smith in the UK. The entries given below are a selection of general yoga magazines:

American Yoga Newsletter. Edited by Linda Cogozzo (Berkeley, CA: Yoga journal). Monthly.
This newsletter is aimed at yoga teachers, particularly those of the Iyengar tradition. It contains a calendar, notes and a resource listing.

Yoga Journal. Edited by Stephen Bodian (Berkeley, CA: California Yoga Teacher's Association). Bi-monthly.
This journal is an attractive publication which includes articles, news, letters and advertisements.

Yoga Today. Edited by Lindy Randall (Lewes: Yoga today). Monthly.
This is a glossy magazine which contains news items, articles and advertisements.

BOOKS

Today, there are thousands of books available throughout the world on yoga. This bibliography is not comprehensive; very specialized items have been omitted but can be tracked down with the aid of the bibliographies mentioned above or by using the more general bibliographies described in Chapter 5. In this section I have included general introductions to the subject.

Bates, C. (1986) *Ransoming the Mind: An Integration of Yoga and Modern Therapy,* YES International Publications, St Paul, MN.
This book looks at the integration of yoga and modern therapy and the meeting ground of the two approaches.
Bender, R. (1975) *Yoga Exercises for Every Body,* Ruben, Avon, Connecticut.
Bender, R. (1978) *Yoga Exercises for More Flexible Bodies,* Ruben, Avon, Connecticut.
Berg, V. (1981) *Yoga in Pregnancy,* Watkins, London.
Bromage, B. (1979) *Tibetan Yoga,* Aquarian, Wellingborough.
Butler, D. G. (1975) *Teaching Yoga,* Pelham, London.
Carr, R. (1973) *Be a Frog, a Bird, or a Tree: Rachel Carr's Creative Yoga Exercises for Children,* Doubleday, New York.
Carr, R. (1980) *See and Be: Yoga and Creative Movement for Children,* Spectrum, Hemel Hempstead.
Haich, E. and Yesudian, S. (1986) *Self Healing, Yoga and Destiny,* Aurora, New York.
Isaacson, C. (1985) *Yoga for All,* Thorsons, Wellingborough.
Iyengar, B. K. S. (1985) *Light on Yoga,* Allen & Unwin, London.
This is a comprehensive manual and gives special mention to the Iyengar method.
Lasater, J. H. (1978) *Yoga and Bodywork,* Grove, New York.
Lidell, L. (1983) *The Book of Yoga,* Ebury, London.
A simple introduction to yoga with many helpful diagrams and photographs.
Peterson, E. (1987) *Yoga Step by Step,* Black, London.
Tobias, M. and Stewart, M. (1987) *The Yoga Book,* Pan, London.
An excellent introduction to this subject: clear, uncluttered and easy to follow.

PART III
PEOPLE, ORGANIZATIONS AND ACTIVITIES

9

Finding out about people, organizations and activities

This chapter provides information and help on finding out about:

People – practitioners, trainers, authors and the like
Informal groups and networks
Societies, associations and therapy centres, and also
Current activities such as workshops and training courses.

PEOPLE

People are a very important information source easily overlooked by anyone carrying out an extensive literature search. Individuals may be able to help by clarifying particular procedures or techniques, or by offering training or consultancy services, individual therapy or healing, information on resources or training courses and so on.

Individuals who may be able to help can be identified in a number of ways:

1   Ask someone (for example other therapists, organizations, magazine editors).
2   Read the current literature to see if anyone is writing about the subject you are interested in.
3   Consult printed directories.

Individuals can be tracked down in a number of ways:

1   Using directories such as the telephone directory or those

mentioned in Chapter 5. Directories should always be used with caution because:

(a) they become out of date rapidly as, for example, people move house or change their field of work

(b) they are not comprehensive and omissions are likely to include individuals who are less well known or do not like advertising in this form, and also those who are relatively new to the field.

2 Contacting informal groups and networks.

3 Contacting organizations and societies.

Methods 2 and 3 are covered below.

4 Attending conferences and workshops. For example, about 200 healers and therapists from around the world attended the Spirit of Healing workshop held at Findhorn, UK in 1987. This was therefore a very useful conference to attend if one wanted to make contacts around the world.

5 Serendipity.

INFORMAL GROUPS AND NETWORKS

In many parts of the UK, and in other countries, therapists and healers come together formally and informally to share resources, training skills and experiences. They may also maintain registers and information files about activities and contacts in their geographic area or field of interest.

An example of a geographic network is the Leeds Healing Network, which is an informal group of therapists and healers who work in the Leeds area of the UK. They produce and distribute the *Leeds Healing Network Internal Register,* an annual publication described in Chapter 5 in the section headed 'Directories'. Therapists and healers in this network cover the following fields:

Acupuncture, Alexander technique, allergy therapy, aroma-therapy, art therapy, autogenics, colour healing, counselling and Rogerian counselling, dance therapy, circle dance, dietary therapy, flower remedies, healing, herbalism, homeopathy, hypnotherapy, massage, meditation, metamorphic technique, naturopath-osteopathy, polarity therapy, postural integration, psychotherapy, rebirthing, reflexology, Reichian therapy, spiritual healing, synergetics, T'ai chi, tarot, and yoga.

The network includes people concerned with many different types of therapy. Networks also exist which are concerned with one particular therapy, for example co-counselling or gestalt therapy. A publication representing a network of people involved in one type of therapy is *Present Time,* which is concerned with re-evaluation co-counselling in the USA. This publication can be used to identify re-evaluation co-counsellors throughout the world.

Informal groups and networks may produce their own newsletter, lists of activities and members, or journals. These can be quite difficult to track down as they are semi-published and tend not to get into traditional guides and directories. They may also be quite short-lived. As many of these publications as it has been possible to track down have been included in either the relevant sections in Chapter 5 or the specialized sources sections but the author recognizes that this book does not provide a comprehensive listing of such publications.

ORGANIZATIONS, SOCIETIES AND THERAPY CENTRES

A diverse collection of organizations are either involved in or likely to be of interest to people concerned with alternative therapy. These organizations include:

International organizations
Government bodies such as health services, social services
Libraries and information units
Professional associations
Education and training bodies
Publishers
Therapy centres
Voluntary organizations.

International organizations

International organizations include traditional bodies such as the World Health Organization (WHO) and professional bodies such as the International Society for Creative Art in Therapy. These bodies can be identified using directories such as:

The Creative Tree. Edited by Gina Levete (Wilton, Salisbury: Michael Russell, 1987).
The directory in this book is international in its coverage, which includes the creative therapies.

and other directories mentioned in Chapters 5 to 8.

Government bodies

Government bodies such as health services and social services contain individuals and groups who may be quite active in the field of alternative therapies. These can be tracked down with the help of professional societies such as the British Association of Counselling and publications such as *Guide to Government Departments and Other Libraries and Information Bureaux.*

Libraries and information units

Libraries and information units are discussed in Chapter 3, and Chapter 5 contains details on how to identify and locate them. Important sources include:

American Library Directory
ASLIB Directory of Information Sources in the United Kingdom
Directory of Special Libraries and Information Centres
Encyclopedia of Information Systems and Services
Libraries in the United Kingdom and the Republic of Ireland
Subject Collections in European Libraries
World Guide to Libraries
World Guide to Special Libraries.

Professional associations

Professional associations are organizations which are set up to support the activities and needs of their members. They frequently provide information services both to their members and the public. Professional associations can be tracked down using guides such as:

Directory of British Associations
Directory of International and National Medical and Related Societies
Encyclopedia of Associations
Yearbook of International Organizations

and others described in Chapters 5 to 8. A typical example is:

Association Française de Musicothérapie
40 rue de Province
75009 Paris

This is a national association which sponsors world conferences and publishes a journal.

Professional associations of other groups such as the British Medical Association occasionally publish materials of relevance to alternative therapists. A good example is the controversial BMA report, widely reported in the press:

Alternative Therapy. Report of the Board of Science and Education (BMA) (London: BMA, 1986).

This report concentrates on the following therapies: acupuncture; aromatherapy; Bach flower remedies; healing; Hellerwork; herbalism; homeopathy; hypnotherapy; iridology; macrobiotics; naturopathy; orthomolecular treatment; osteopathy and chiropractic; polarity therapy; radionics; reflexology. It briefly covers legal issues both in the UK and parts of Europe and it includes a brief bibliography.

Education and training bodies

Traditional institutions can be identified using sources such as:

American Universities and Colleges, 12th edn (New York: American Council on Education, 1983).

189

British Qualifications: A Comprehensive Guide to Educational, Technical, Professional and Academic Qualifications in Britain, 14th edn (London: Kogan Page, 1983).

Commonwealth Universities Yearbook: A Directory to the Universities of the Commonwealth and the Handbook of Their Association (London: Association of Commonwealth Universities). Annual.

Directory of Technical and Further Education (London: George Goodwin). Irregular.

Graduate Studies: A Guide to Postgraduate Study in the UK (Cambridge: Hobsons). Annual.

International Handbook of Universities: And Other Institutions of Higher Education, 10th edn (Paris: International Association of Universities, 1986). Every three years.

The World of Learning (London: Europa). Annual.

Independent educational and training bodies can be identified using sources such as:

Bear's Guide to Non-Traditional College Degrees, 9th edn. By John Bear (Berkeley, CA: Celestial Arts, 1986/7).

The Creative Tree. Edited by Gina Levete (Wilton, Salisbury: Michael Russell, 1987).

DITTO. Directory of Independent Training and Tutorial Bodies. By Elizabeth Summerson and Maureen Davies (Richmond: Career Consultants Ltd, 1985).

Getting into Alternative Medicine and Therapies. By Elizabeth J Summerson (Richmond, Surrey: Career Consultants, 1985).

Thorsons' Complete Guide to Alternative Living. By David Harvey (Wellingborough: Thorsons, 1986).

These independent bodies can also be tracked down using periodicals and magazines such as:

Here's Health
Human Potential
Yoga Today.

These are detailed in Chapters 5 to 8.

Publishers

Publishers can be identified by going into either a bookshop or library and looking at items by a particular publisher, so obtaining the address, or by using the directories listed in Chapter 5.

Therapy centres

Therapy centres can be identified by using guides such as:

The Directory of Complementary and Alternative Practitioners. 1987–88. Compiled and edited by Michael C. Williams (Colyton, Devon: Health Farm Publishing, 1987–).

Handbuch zur Information und Kontaktaufnahme in der Alternativen Szene. Compiled by Das Addressbuch Alternativer Projekte (Klingelbach, West Germany: Mandala Verlag Peter Meyer). Annual.

The Institute of Complementary Medicine Yearbook (London: Foulsham, 1986–).

New Consciousness Sourcebook. By Parmatma Singh Khalsa (Berkeley, CA: Spiritual Community Publications, 1982).

A Pilgrim's Guide to Planet Earth. Edited by Parmatma Singh Khalsa (San Rafael, CA: Spiritual Community Publications, 1981).

Thorsons' Complete Guide to Alternative Living. By David Harvey (Wellingborough: Thorsons, 1986).

These directories are all described in detail in Chapter 5. Therapy centres can also be identified using periodicals such as those listed below in 'Finding out about current activities'.

Voluntary organizations

A variety of voluntary organizations are concerned with therapy frequently in the context of self-help therapy. They vary in size from an individual working from home to a group with full-time employees, and in the type of assistance they can offer. This may be financial help, counselling and therapy, or support via a self-help group. As these organizations frequently depend on voluntary help they may be short-lived. Organizations such as the Citizens Advice Bureau in the UK (local branches are listed in the telephone directory) frequently maintain files of voluntary bodies, as do many public libraries.

These organizations can also be tracked down using standard directories such as *Directory of British Associations* and *Encyclopedia of Associations*, and also specialized directories such as the *Someone to Talk to Directory*. These directories are all described in Chapter 5.

FINDING OUT ABOUT CURRENT ACTIVITIES

There is a variety of methods of finding out about activities, for example workshops or training courses in a particular subject or geographic area.

1 Direct contact with a society – many specialist societies and organizations produce newsletters and listings of activities in their field, and can be tracked down using the directories and other tools to searching which are described above.
2 Use of general magazines – a number of magazines contain listings of activities. Important examples in the UK include:

Cahoots
Creative Mind
Here's Health
Human Potential
Link Up
One Earth
Resurgence.

3 Use of specialist magazines such as those listed in Chapters 6 to 8 under the particular types of therapy. Examples include:

Out from the Core
Shaman's Drum
Stroking Times
Yoga Today.

4 Advertisements in therapy centres, whole-food shops and other places.
5 Many workshops are not advertised in printed publications but through local outlets such as shops and therapy centres.

Index

This is a combined author, subject and title index. Authors' names (including corporate bodies) and subject headings are presented in lower case. Organizations mentioned in the text are presented in upper case. Titles are presented in lower case and in italics. All references are to page numbers.

The index is sorted into letter by letter alphabetical order. Numbers appear at the beginning of the sequence.

195

206

Index